THE
BIBLE QUIZ BOOK

by

Frederick Hall

BAKER BOOK HOUSE
Grand Rapids, Michigan

ISBN: 0-8010-4057-4

Seventh printing, January 1984

Copyright 1943 by
Baker Book House Company

Previously published under the title
The Family Bible Quiz Book

PHOTOLITHOPRINTED BY CUSHING - MALLOY, INC.
ANN ARBOR, MICHIGAN, UNITED STATES OF AMERICA

CONTENTS

NOTE: Unless otherwise stated, all direct quotations from the Bible are taken from either the Authorized or the American Standard Revision.

DEDICATION AND FOREWORD
To L. H. R.

My Dear Grandson:

On your birthday cake this month, there was just *one* candle. How can any person, even one as wise as a grandfather is supposed to be, make a book for so small a boy and be sure it will please him when he grows up? It is quite impossible, though on this one I have tried my best. Still, it may help a little if I tell you something about it—at least what to look for and what to skip.

The "What-Happened-Next?" stories your mother will soon be reading to you. You may like them—I hope you will. Some of the "Honest-Serving-Men" questions you may learn as you hear them over and over. That name was given them because in the *Just-so Stories*, which you will hear some day, Mr. Kipling says:

> I keep six honest serving men
>   (They taught me all I knew);
> Their names are What and Why and When
>   And How and Where and Who.

These Honest Serving Men are very useful. Mr. Kipling found them so, he tells us. They have given me much help and very soon you will be working them night and day.

The questions from there on get harder and you will be a most unusual boy if you can answer many of them before you are in your teens. Those in the last part of the book ——! If I were in your place, I would not bother with them at all until you are well into High School. Try them, if you like, on your father and mother but, wise as they are, you must not expect them to know all the answers. Even your grandfather would have trouble answering all the questions, if he had not made them up himself.

One serious thing, here in the ending of my letter to you: as I have said, whether you are going to like my book or not, I do not know. But I am quite certain that some day you will love the book my book is about. (Not all parts of it equally of course, for no sensible person loves any book that way.) I never saw any one who really knew the Bible who did not love it and most people love it more and more as they grow older and come to know it better. Getting acquainted with it is like coming to know a kind, interesting and helpful friend.

Your loving grandfather,
FREDERICK HALL.

Berea, Kentucky.

ALL-AGE BIBLE QUIZZES

Section I
"WHAT HAPPENED NEXT?"

No. 1. A HUNGRY FAMILY

Jacob's whole family—and it was a large family—was greatly worried and all of the men met together to decide what to do. There had been no crops that year nor the year before. They had tried to ration their food carefully but it was running very low and they saw that, unless they could get more somewhere—and soon, their wives and children would have nothing to eat.

Food was to be found, they knew, in Egypt: they knew because they had once been there and a Great Man had given them some. But he had kept one of their brothers, as a sort of "hostage," and he had told them that they would get nothing more from him unless on their next trip they brought their youngest brother, Benjamin. But their father Jacob loved Benjamin dearly and said they simply should not take him.

" If we don't," they answered, " there is no need of our going at all. We won't be able even to see the Great Man. He told us so. We may as well stay right here at home and starve."

You can imagine how every day they saw their stock of food growing less and less and how again and again they talked it over until finally ——

What happened next?

No. 2. THE MAN BESIDE THE WELL

One day seven young women who were sisters went to a well to water some sheep that belonged to their father, who seems to have been an important man for, besides keeping sheep, the Bible tells us he was also a priest. They drew water and filled the troughs so that the sheep could drink and then some men, who were shepherds and wanted their own sheep to drink first, came up and drove the girls away. At least they started to do it but they did not get far because, much to their surprise, and probably to the surprise of the girls too, a young man sitting beside the well jumped up and drove *them* away. He did not know the girls, he had never seen them before but he was that kind of man. When he saw an injustice, he simply had to do something about it. The girls watered their sheep, thanked him (at least I suppose they thanked him) and went home. Then ——

What happened next?

No. 3. A FAMOUS GREAT-GRANDMOTHER

This story is about two women who were not really related but were great friends and, though it begins sadly, in the end it comes out all right.

The older woman, whose name was Naomi, had grown up and married near the town of Bethlehem, where many years later Jesus was to be born. In her day it was just one of many little villages: no one dreamed it would ever become world famous. Hard times came to Bethlehem, as they are apt to come to any community. It was difficult to get enough to eat and so finally she and her husband took their two boys and moved into a foreign country, where they hoped to do better. For the same reason, in our own time, many people have come to *our* country. There the boys grew up and married and then they and her husband died.

Left alone, except for her two daughters-in-law, Naomi remembered her old home town where now, she heard, they had good times again, and she decided to go back. Her daughters-in-law said they would go with her but she told them no: they would be happier, she thought, if they stayed in their own country.

What happened next?

No. 4. A SOLDIER'S DREAM

Two armies faced each other: one so large that the Bible says

[Answers on pages 28–29]

the men seemed like grasshoppers, the other small—so very small it did not look as if it had a chance of winning. The commander of the little army was named Gideon and, though he was a brave man, it would not be surprising if he found the outlook discouraging.

Then one night with his servant (in a modern army he would probably be called an orderly) he set out on a scouting expedition toward the camp of the enemy. He wanted to see for himself exactly how the land lay. Presently they were within the enemy's lines and crouching down outside a tent in which two common soldiers were talking. They lay listening intently and what they heard was something like this:

"You know ——" This was the first soldier. "Last night I had a queer dream—the queerest dream I ever had. I thought a loaf of bread—just an ordinary loaf of barley bread—came tumbling down the hill into our camp. It hit a tent and—believe it or not!—it knocked it over. The tent lay flat along the ground. You think a dream like that could mean anything?"

"Well ——" said the other soldier.

What happened next?

No. 5. THE SURPRISED YOUNG MAN

The whole people of Israel was troubled. Samuel, who for years had been their judge, was grown an old man and could no longer govern them as wisely as he had once done. His sons had been appointed to do some of his work but they were not good men and the people did not trust them. Also, the land was surrounded by powerful enemies, who were constantly making war on them and the people knew that, if they did not defend themselves, they would soon be destroyed or made slaves. There should, they thought, be a change in their kind of government and it ought to be made at once.

Still, the work of every day, the fishing, and farming, the selling, and buying, the weaving, and sheep-tending, had to go on much as usual and, one morning when a farmer named Kish rose and found that some of his animals had strayed away, he spoke to his son Saul about it and Saul, a tall, fine looking young man, took one of the servants and set off to see if he could find them.

[Answers on page 29]   9

They were gone several days, so long in fact that the father began to worry about *them*. They hunted far and wide, they asked questions of every one they met and, for all their pains, they never really found the animals they were after but, when they had gone a long way, they came to Samuel's city and ——

What happened next?

No. 6. THE BOY WITH FIVE STONES

Many times you have heard about the hero of this story but did you ever hear about his brother Eliab?

King Saul had gathered his men to fight the Philistines, with whom he was always having trouble, and Eliab and the two brothers next younger were at the front but for a long time nothing had been doing there and this all because of one man. He was an enormously big Philistine who each day would come out and dare any man in the other army to fight him. But no one liked the idea of fighting a giant and so in the Jewish army morale sank lower and lower.

Then one day, who should appear in camp but Eliab's youngest brother, too young to be drafted, who commonly stayed at home to look after the sheep. Their father had sent something for his soldier sons to eat (something for their captain too) and wanted to learn how they were getting on.

Eliab and the others were glad enough to get the food from home—that is something soldiers always welcome—but, when they found the boy was asking a lot of questions about the Philistine champion, Eliab was angry, partly, I think (though he did not admit it), because he knew his little brother pretty well and was afraid he might run into danger. He scolded him good and hard and then ——

What happened next?

No. 7. THE SPENT ARROWS

David, now a young soldier, was in great danger. He had been in King Saul's court and had served him faithfully but Saul had become insanely jealous of him (really insane) and wanted to kill him. He might have succeeded too, had it not been for

10 [Answers on pages 29–30]

Saul's son, Prince Jonathan, who loved David and was determined that no harm should come to him.

One day they met in a safe place and talked everything over and it was decided that, for the present, it was better that David should stay in hiding. Meanwhile Jonathan would learn what he could and get word to him, if it was safe for him to return to the court.

Then one day a boy who knew Prince Jonathan met him carrying his bow and arrows and the prince ——

What happened next?

No. 8. THE PROPHET'S STORY

About the hardest thing any man can have to do is to go to a friend whom he loves dearly and say to him, " You have done a bad thing and God is going to punish you for it." Yet the command to do just this was once laid upon the prophet Nathan and the man to whom he was sent was his friend, King David.

We can imagine how he thought it over: " It can do little good to tell him what I or any one else thinks. Kings do not enjoy hearing such things and the chances are it would only make him angry. If I can, I must make him see for himself just how bad he has been. What now is the best way to go about it? "

Finally he remembered (or so I think) how years ago the king had been a shepherd boy. So he went to him and told him a story, something like this:

" Once upon a time, there were two men. One was very rich, with many flocks and herds; the other was poor—he had just one pet lamb and —— Well, *you* know how fond a man can be of a pet lamb. One day a guest came to the rich man's house. He wanted to serve him something especially good for dinner and ——"

What happened next?

No. 9. THE YOUNG KING'S DREAM

King David lived to be an old man but he died at last and, in his place, his son Solomon came to the throne. Sometimes we thoughtlessly talk about being " as happy as kings " but, for

Solomon, those first days of kingship must have been anxious and troubled. Not all of his people were his friends: some, as he knew well, would rather have been ruled by his brother Adonijah. Compared with some neighboring kingdoms, his was not rich. Also, the rulers of some of these kingdoms were enemies, who would have liked nothing better than a chance to invade and conquer his country. He might be called to fight them but, unlike his father, young Solomon had never had any experience as a soldier. Neither had he had much experience as a statesman. All of his counsellors wanted to stand well with him but none of them knew nor did he himself know how wise and able a king he was going to be. We can imagine how day after day he thought of these things. He thought of them so much that finally one night he dreamed about them.

He dreamed that God came to him and they talked together, as he might have talked with his father, David. "Solomon," God said, "what would you like to have me give you?"

And Solomon answered ——

What happened next?

No. 10. THE FOOD THAT LASTED

Once upon a time, a poor woman, whose husband was dead, was gathering wood to build a fire and cook what she thought would be the last meal that she and her little boy would ever eat. She was busy picking up sticks and trying to forget her sorrow, when looking up she saw a passing stranger, who asked her if she would give him a drink of water.

Gladly, she told him: she would get it right away. Then, as she turned to go, he called again and asked her if she would bring him something to eat too. She came back then and explained. There had been no rain for a long time, she told him, and it did not look as if there would be anything to gather at the next harvest time. Meanwhile all the food they had saved up had gradually disappeared. She had not wasted anything. She had been as careful as she could but now only enough was left for one more meal. When she and her little boy had eaten it, she saw nothing for it but they would have to starve.

12   [Answers on page 31]

" I see," said the strange man. " Well, cook your meal for yourself and your son but first——"
What happened next?

No. 11. THE LITTLE CLOUD

A great gathering had been held on Mount Carmel—a mountain in the Holy Land, which overlooks the sea.

Many people of the land had been worshipping an idol called Baal. The prophet Elijah wanted them to worship God and he thought that a great gathering and a sort of vote would decide the matter. So they met, in a sort of contest, which was decided in Elijah's favor, though he was but one man, with many rival priests arrayed against him. It had been an exciting day and a hard day but he had won and we can imagine his feeling that, from now on, everything was going to be all right. The people would believe what he had long been telling them and would turn from their silly idols and worship the true God.

There remained one thing however: one thing more. For long months there had been no rain and he had promised the king, whose name was Ahab, that God would send it today. With his one servant, he went up to the top of Mount Carmel and——
What happened next?

No. 12. THE PATRIOT

It was a time of great trouble. Enemies had over-run and conquered the country once ruled by David and Solomon and had carried away many of the people as prisoners. Still, this did not mean that God had forgotten them or that all of the exiles were unhappy. In the land of their captivity some of them had found better homes than those they had left behind. Others found new trades, which they enjoyed more than the callings they had followed before—farming, fishing and sheep-raising. Some became scholars, which none of them had ever been before. A few became rich and prosperous and one of these was a man named Nehemiah, who lived at the court and was the king's cupbearer —a very important office, though you might not think it. He certainly, you would say, should have been contented. What could trouble *him?* But one day some one came to him from his old home and told him how poor and miserable and unprotected were the people still living there, how no one was doing anything for them and they were even squabbling among themselves. It disturbed Nehemiah. A long time he thought it over sadly and then ——

What happened next?

No. 13. THE MAN WHO TRIED TO RUN AWAY FROM GOD

That God is everywhere is something that we learn only as we grow older. Once you yourself, perhaps, thought of God as living in the church. Did not people call it " God's house " ? And, if some one had said, " God can hear you, and help you, and speak to you, just as easily in the woods, or in your own home," it might have seemed strange to you.

Long ago, before people had come to understand as much about God as they do now, it would have seemed so even to grown up people for many of them then thought of each country (say, Mexico, the United States and Canada) as having a god all of its own. Something like this seems to have been in the mind of a man named Jonah, who should have known better, for he worshipped the true God: only he seems to have had little idea of his greatness.

God wanted him to preach in a certain city—of that he was very sure—but he was even surer that he did not want to do it. It was a large, wicked city. He did not like its people and, worse still, he did not want them to be sorry for their wickedness—he *wanted* God to punish them. Now that, as Jesus taught us, is no way for any man to feel about even his worst enemies but Jonah did feel that way.

" If," he thought, " I could only run away from God and hide somewhere! "

What happened next?

No. 14. THE PRAYER JESUS GAVE

Long ago, in Bible times, a wonderful experience came to

14   [Answers on page 32]

twelve quite ordinary men who lived in Galilee. A friend asked them to give up their regular work and go with him about the country, talking to people, preaching to them, helping them. In the beginning, they perhaps thought of him as just one of themselves. Some of them earned their livings with boats and fishing nets, while he earned his living with saw and hammer. But it was not long before they began to see a great difference between him and all other men and they came to call him, " Master."

They saw him heal sick people in a way that they could not understand at all. They heard him tell the most wonderful and beautiful stories that any man ever told. They saw him with friends and with enemies, with rich people and poor people, in crowds and in homes where he and they were being entertained. They heard him comfort people in trouble and warn people in danger. They heard him pray to God and that may well have been the most wonderful experience of all, for he called God, " Our Father," and talked to him as if they were well acquainted. " Why can't *we* talk to God that way? " they must have asked themselves. Finally, one day they went to him and said " Master, John the Baptist taught his disciples to pray. Won't you teach us? "

What happened next?

No. 15.   THE MESSAGE FROM PRISON

Before Jesus began preaching and teaching, another man, whom we call John the Baptist, told the Jewish people that the Kingdom of God was coming and that they ought to get ready for it. The crowds that came to hear him were so much moved that they wondered if he himself were not the man who would bring in God's Kingdom but he told them no: he was only preparing the way for some one who would come after him. Later, he saw Jesus and in him recognized the man whom God had chosen.

Then, suddenly, John had to stop preaching. A wicked king put him in prison and, shut up there—he who had lived all his life out of doors—he grew troubled, discouraged and uncertain, just as at times all of us do. Had he been mistaken? God, he was sure, would send *some* one but was Jesus the one? How could he be sure?

We can imagine how, day after day, he thought about it, how at night alone in his prison cell he brooded over it, how perhaps he talked about it with friends who came to visit him. You see, he had heard strange and contradictory rumors about Jesus and they puzzled and troubled him. Finally ——

What happened next?

No. 16. THE BLIND MAN

When Jesus was upon earth, there were some men (and we have some still) who wanted to bring all life down to a set of rules. Then you would be " good," if you kept the rules and " bad," if you did not keep them. They said that was the way to live and to decide everything. One of their rules was that no work should be done on the Sabbath—no work of *any* sort. Now, if some one in your family is very sick, the doctor comes on Sunday, just as he would come on any other day and Jesus did the same thing—he helped sick people on the Sabbath. But the people who were so strong for rules said that was very wrong.

One day he saw a blind man and his disciples thought the man (or else his parents) must have been very wicked: otherwise why should he be blind? But Jesus told them we have no right, because a man is in trouble, to think that his trouble came as a punishment. Then he healed the blind man and ——

What happened next?

No. 17. THE BOY WHO LEFT HOME

This is the most famous short story in the world—a story Jesus once told his friends to teach them how God thinks of us and how we ought to think of him.

A father, he said, had two sons, and the younger boy became uneasy. He had a good home. His father was always kind to him but he found home life dull and monotonous. He wanted to get away where things were " doing." One day he told his father so and his father was not greatly surprised, nor did he say, " Now, see here! I'm your father. You'll do what I say." He

16   [Answers on page 33]

did not even argue with him. He seems to have thought, " It's no use to tell him. He will have to find out for himself. Some day perhaps he will come back—I hope he will."

So the boy went away and, just as he had expected, he had a " great " time—that is he did as long as his money lasted. When that was gone, he found his friends were gone too. He had to do hard, disagreeable work in order to get anything to eat and at last he was feeding hogs and so hungry he was ready to eat what the hogs ate.

What happened next?

No. 18.   THE BROTHER WHO WAS NOT GLAD

This goes on with the story that Jesus told about the boy who went away into a far country and spent all his money there and then came home, having found out that after all home was the best place. You remember how glad his father was when he came back. *This* story is about the boy's older brother, who never went away but stayed quietly at home. What work he had to do he did regularly and, if his father ever worried about him, it was not because of any foolish things he did—things of a sort to set the neighbors talking. He was never " wild ": he was always steady and dependable.

On the day that his brother came home, he had been out in the fields as usual. Toward evening he quit work and started back. I imagine he was tired and hungry. As he came in sight of the house, he noticed that something quite unusual was happening. So he called a servant and asked him about it. " Why, hadn't you heard? " the man said. " Your brother has come home and your father is giving a party for him."

What happened next?

No. 19.   THE WEDDING OF THE KING'S SON

Nearly all of Jesus' stories were about ordinary people. He told about farmers sowing and reaping their fields, about shepherds caring for their sheep, women house-cleaning, fishermen emptying their nets and sorting out the fish. But the scene of this story is a king's court.

[Answers on pages 33–34]   **17**

The king's son, it seems, was to be married and, as you can imagine, great preparations were being made. Among other things, there was to be a splendid feast and, when it was ready, the king sent out his servants (that seems to have been the custom of the time) to tell those invited that the dinner was now ready—come and eat it.

Then something happened that is almost unbelievable. You would think that any one would be glad to go to a party, especially if a king had invited them, but the people who were invited to this wedding —— Not only did they stay away, they made fun of it and even mistreated the poor servants who had come to invite them.

The king of course was angry (kings are not used to being treated that way). He punished them and then ——

What happened next?

No. 20. THE TWO HOUSES

In the far-off times of Abraham, Isaac and Jacob, the Jewish people lived in tents that could be easily taken down and moved from place to place. But, in Jesus' time, they had for hundreds of years been living in houses as we do, though of course not exactly the same kind of houses. Theirs were built mostly of stone and had flat roofs—you have seen pictures of them. Jesus himself probably helped to build such houses for, as you will remember, when a young man he worked at the trade of a carpenter.

This story, which he once told his disciples, is about two houses that, so far as we know, were exactly alike—except for one thing. The outside walls, the roof, the partitions, the floors —all were, apparently, of just as good material and just as well put together in one house as in the other but there was one important difference. One had a foundation that went down to " bed rock." The other was built on nothing more solid than a sand bank. Then, when both were finished ——

What happened next?

     [Answers on page 34]

No. 21. LONG AND SHORT TIME WORKERS

Here is a story that Jesus told about a man who owned a vine-yard.

It was a busy time, he needed extra men and, going out into the market place, he hired some whom he found there and told them just what he would pay them. About nine o'clock, he went out again, saw other men waiting and told them, if they would go to his vineyard, he would pay them whatever was right. Again at twelve and at three he went, each time hiring more men. Finally, about five, he went once more and, finding still other men who were idle, and learning that no one had hired them, he said:

" You too go and work in my vineyard."

At evening he told his foreman, " Pay the men off. Begin with those who came in last." They stood ready to be paid off and ——

What happened next?

No. 22. WEEDS AND WHEAT

Jesus once told his friends a story about a farmer who sowed a field of wheat and was looking forward to reaping a good crop, when an enemy did a very mean thing. He came at night when the farmer was asleep and all over the field he sowed the seeds of weeds. (Your Bible may call them " tares " but that is just another name for weeds.)

The seeds were too small to be noticed and for a time no one knew what had happened. But, as they began to grow, they did not look like wheat stalks and the man's servants came to him and said:

" That seed we sowed in your field was good seed, wasn't it? "

He said yes and then, when they went on to tell him about the weeds that were springing up everywhere, he thought a minute and realized what must have happened—an enemy had done it.

" Shall we go out into the field and pull up all the weeds? " his servants asked him.

What happened next?

[Answers on pages 34–35]   19

No. 23. THE MAN WHO WAS GOING TO
ENJOY HIMSELF

Did you ever think it would be no end of fun to have everything you wanted? Go into the biggest restaurant in any city and pick out whatever you liked to eat and drink? Go into a store and buy anything you pleased? No one to tell you what you must or must not do? Anything you liked!

It might not be so much fun as you think. At least it turned out badly for a man in one of the stories that Jesus told.

He was a farmer and he had had a very good year. When they began gathering in his crops, he saw right away that his barns were not going to be big enough to hold them. " Where can I put them all? " he thought and decided the thing to do was to pull down his barns and build bigger ones. In them he would put his " goods " and then he would say to himself, " Just look at all you've got! Now have a good time—eat all you want to —drink all you want to—enjoy yourself." But he didn't, because ——

What happened next?

No. 24. FATHER AND SONS

Boys, I suspect, have been pretty much alike always, no matter in what country they lived or how long ago. Here is a story that Jesus told about a father who had two sons and it is just the sort of thing that might have happened yesterday to some one you know.

The father owned a vineyard and, at a time when a lot of work was needed there, he hunted up his older boy and said to him:

" Son, go work in my vineyard."

He must have been a queer sort of boy or at least in a queer mood for—believe it or not!—he turned round to his father and said:

" I will not."

That of course was no way for any boy to talk but, apparently, the father did not scold him or even stop to argue with him. He just went on and afterward, as you might expect, the boy got to thinking about it. He saw how rude and disobedient he had

[Answers on pages 35–36]

been. He remembered too that he himself ought to be interested in seeing the vineyard do well. I imagine that, as he thought about it, he was pretty much ashamed of himself. At any rate, he hurried off to the vineyard and put in a good day's work there.

Meanwhile, the father had hunted up his other son and had asked him to do the work. He said sure (or something like that) but ——

What happened next?

No. 25.   THE MAN WHO WAS UNFORGIVING

Suppose you had a friend who, every once in a while, would "fly off the handle" and do or say something he ought not to but who was always sorry for it afterward and would come and say so. How long ought you to have to put up with a friend like that? Should you finally say to him: "Now, see here! I'm through. I've forgiven you now for the last time."

Jesus said no: there must never be a "last time." Then he told this story:

A rich king once loaned his servants a great deal of money— to one of them as much as ten million dollars. (Goodspeed's translation.) One day he wanted the money back and asked the man for it but the man could not pay it. The king started to try to collect it but the man begged hard, promising that he would pay it back some time and finally the king said, "Oh, well—let it go." Then ——

What happened next?

No. 26.   THE MAN WHO WAS SLEEPY

Here is a story Jesus told his friends and I think he must have smiled when he told it, for it is a rather funny story, though what it teaches is serious enough.

Once upon a time, he said, there was a man who had an unexpected visitor. A friend came to him in the middle of the night. The friend had been travelling, he was tired and hungry and, naturally, the man wanted to feed him but, when he went to the cupboard, he found it as bare as Old Mother Hubbard's.

"What in the world am I going to do?" he asked himself.

Then he remembered his next door neighbor. He would surely have something, even if at times he was " grouchy " about doing favors. So, rushing over there, he began pounding on the door. The neighbor woke up and called out to ask the reason of all the noise.

" A friend has come to me," the man said and went on to explain his trouble.

" Oh, dear me! " the neighbor said. (Not just these words of course.) " I'm sleepy. I can't bother to get up and find food for this friend of yours. He isn't *my* friend: I don't even know him. Won't you please go away and not bother me any more? "

And then——

What happened next?

No. 27. THE MAN WHO CLIMBED A TREE

Long ago, in a city called Jericho, there lived a man whose name was Zacchaeus. He was rich and he had powerful friends among the Romans, the real rulers of his country; in fact he helped them collect the taxes but his own people hated him and, were he living today, he would probably be called by some bad name like fifth columnist. I'm afraid too that he would deserve the name. One thing more about him—he was a short man: no taller, perhaps, than a boy of twelve or thirteen.

He had heard about Jesus, his teaching, his healings, his kindness to all sorts of people, even those who held jobs that were not considered quite respectable. " He must be a remarkable person," he thought. " It is not of course to be expected that he would have anything to do with a man like me—I know what people say about *my* job!—but, if ever I get the chance, I am going to see him."

Then one day his chance came.

" He is here," some one told him. " Right in our city! In a few minutes, he will be going down that street."

He rushed out into a street that was packed with people and there his first glance told him that so short a man as he could not possibly get within sight of Jesus, too many other people wanted

22   [Answers on page 37]

to see him. So he ran ahead and climbed up into a tree, from
which he could look down as they passed.

What happened next?

No. 28. THE MAN IN THE COURTYARD

Jesus had many powerful enemies. He knew that one day
these enemies would take him and kill him and he tried to prepare his disciples for that troubled time but they were perfectly
sure that they would always be faithful to him, no matter what
happened. They all told him so and Peter, in particular, said
that, even if every other man were disloyal, he himself never
would be—he would die first. That was like Peter, quick to
promise but not seeing very far ahead, and Jesus warned him but
Peter simply could not believe his warning.

Then something happened more dreadful than he or any of
them could possibly have imagined. Rough men arrested their
master and dragged him into court. He was insulted and ill-
treated, accused of things he had never done and the power that
they had so often seen him use for others—he never once used it
for himself.

In a panic they ran away but Peter followed afar off, looking
perhaps for a miracle, thinking perhaps that he might still be of
some help. At any rate, he wanted to see how this terrible thing
was going to come out. He got far enough to be one of the
crowd that thronged the courtyard of the palace where the trial
was going on. Then ——

What happened next?

No. 29. A FOOT-RACE

When we are in trouble, we go to our friends. So it was nat-
ural that, in the time of the deepest sorrow that they had ever
known, Peter and John should have found each other.

For three years they had followed the greatest man they had
ever known, hearing his wonderful words, seeing his wonderful
deeds and believing confidently (though he himself had said some
puzzling things hard to be understood) that one day he would be

[Answers on pages 37–38]   23

a king, would deliver them from the Romans and would rule with splendor in Jerusalem.

He was dead now. Their own eyes had seen his cruel death. They had seen him buried. A detail of soldiers had been set to guard the place. The morning of the third day was now come and still they could not realize it. It was like a dream too terrible to be believed. They had no plans. What was left? Unless to go back to the fishing by which they had earned their living, in the days before they knew him.

Then, while they walked and talked together, there came running a woman whom they knew and told them ——

What happened next?

No. 30.   THE MAN WHO WAS PUZZLED

Many years ago, a man who had been up to the temple in Jerusalem to worship was returning and, while riding along in his chariot through a desert country, read aloud to himself. He was a rich man and of great influence, for he was the treasurer of an African kingdom ruled over by a queen named Candace. However, he did not serve the heathen gods of that country: he worshipped the same God that we do and the book he was reading was a part of our Bible, a chapter out of the prophecy of Isaiah. (If your Bible says Esaias, that is really the same name.)   It told of a sheep led to the slaughter, a lamb dumb before its shearers, and it puzzled him. That it had an important meaning he felt sure but *what?*   Then he noticed, walking along beside the chariot, a man he had not seen before and the man looked up and said ——

What happened next?

No. 31.   PETER'S DREAM

One thing that Jesus found it hard to make his disciples understand was that, while race, language, color of skin and the like often make a great difference to *us*, they make no difference at all to God and that, as we grow more and more like him, they will mean less and less to us.

Peter had often heard Jesus say things like this but he seems

24   [Answers on pages 38–39]

not to have understood it fully, until one day when, in a strange city in the home of a friend, he had a dream—a vision, he called it.

He saw something like a great sheet let down out of the sky. In it were a number of animals and a voice told him to kill anything he liked and eat it. Peter was very hungry but he said no—some of the things in that sheet were "unclean." (Which does not mean at all what you would mean by "dirty.") Then the voice told him that he was wrong and he wakened—wondering.

A little later came some visitors, asking for him and ——
What happened next?

No. 32. A GIRL NAMED RHODA

In the troubled time that followed Jesus' passing from the earth, when his friends were trying to carry on his work and enemies were trying to stop them, there lived a wicked ruler named Herod. He cared nothing about Jesus' teaching, one way or the other, but he liked to be popular and, when he found that some people were pleased by his persecution of Jesus' followers, he carried it further and finally arrested Peter and put him in prison.

Peter's friends knew it would do little good to go to law about it. Herod would do just what he pleased anyway. But one thing they could do—they could pray. It might seem best to God that Peter should not remain in prison but should be returned to them. One night they had met in a home where they often gathered. We can imagine how, one after another, they prayed earnestly. Then, suddenly, a silence fell upon them. There was a knock and doubtless some of them were frightened, thinking it might be Herod's police come to arrest them too. A girl named Rhoda finally tiptoed to the door to listen and ——
What happened next?

No. 33. THE PERSECUTOR

When Jesus was gone from the earth and his friends began telling other people about him, many tried to stop them and one of

[Answers on page 39]

those who tried hardest was a young man named Saul, about whom many good things may be said. He had been well brought up and had been given a good education. He was desperately in earnest too. Only it never occurred to him that the followers of Jesus might be right and he himself mistaken. They were not only wrong, he said; they ought to know it. If they did not know it, they ought to be stopped anyhow. He himself would see to it. So he went about having both men and women arrested and, if they would not take back what they had been saying, he had them thrown into prison.

But he was dealing with people even more in earnest than he was and more certain that they were right. So he was not able to stop the spread of the new doctrine. When he had begun to think that he was making some progress in Jerusalem, he learned that it was being preached in other cities and, more determined than ever, he started to stamp it out there.

Taking with him an escort of police, he started for Damascus —he was not going to stand for any more of this. Then ——
What happened next?

No. 34. THE SHRINE MAKER

Long ago, in a great and beautiful city of the olden time, there lived a man whose name was Demetrius. In that day, the people of his city had never heard about Jesus but worshipped a pagan goddess whom they called Diana and for whom they had built a temple so lovely that it was called one of the seven wonders of the world. From distant lands people came to visit the city, the name of which was Ephesus. Many doubtless made it a sort of religious pilgrimage and often, when leaving, they bought little silver shrines to take home with them as souvenirs. Now the shrines were made by Demetrius and some of his friends and they found it a very profitable business.

Then one day Paul came to the city and began telling people about Jesus. It is not certain that Demetrius ever heard Paul preach but he heard about him and he became alarmed.

" Why," he thought, " suppose men go to believing on Jesus and worship *him!* They will stop worshipping Diana! Stop coming to her temple! "

26   [Answers on pages 39–40]

But that, for him, was not the worst of it. For all his talk, he does not seem to have really cared so much about " the great goddess Diana." What really troubled him was that people might stop buying the shrines he made. He brooded and brooded over it, becoming more and more frightened, the longer he brooded, until finally ——

What happened next?

No. 35. THE SHIPWRECK

A company of prisoners were to be taken to Rome by sea and an officer named Julius was in command. When they started, everything looked favorable, but hardly were they in the open before a northwesterly gale swept down upon them and they had to run before it.

To save the ship from being overwhelmed in the waves, they threw out a large part of the cargo and then some of the rigging but even that did not help much. The sky was overcast, the clouds so heavy that, for days, they could see neither sun, moon, nor stars. They did not know where the storm was driving them and they began to feel there was no hope, the ship would certainly be wrecked and they themselves drowned. However, though few of them realized it, they had on board, among their prisoners, one man more important than the ship's captain or the Roman officer and ——

What happened next?

ANSWERS

Section I

"WHAT HAPPENED NEXT?"

No. 1. A HUNGRY FAMILY

Something *had* to be done and Jacob at last agreed to let Benjamin go. Taking him, they went down into Egypt. There they made an amazing discovery. The Great Man in charge of the food distribution was their brother Joseph, whom years before they had wickedly sold into slavery. But he was not angry with them. Instead, he told them to come down into Egypt—all of them—and live there and he would see that they had enough to eat as long as the food shortage lasted.

You will find the whole story in the last chapters of Genesis.

No. 2. THE MAN BESIDE THE WELL

Naturally, they told their father about it and he said, "What! You say this young stranger helped you and you did not ask him to come home with you and have something to eat? Go right back to the well and look for him. Perhaps he is still there." So they went back, and found him, and brought him home with them. In talking with him, their father learned that his name was Moses and that he was in their country because he had fled from the anger of Pharaoh of Egypt. An arrangement was made for him to stay on with them and, just as you might have expected, he married one of the sisters.

You will find the whole story in Exodus 2.

No. 3. A FAMOUS GREAT-GRANDMOTHER

One of them, named Orpah, did stay; but the other, whose name was Ruth, said she was going to go wherever Naomi went.

28

(Naomi must have been a very good woman to have some one not really related to her love her that much.) So they went back together and the end of the story tells us how in Bethlehem Ruth was married again to a good man named Boaz. Their first baby, Obed, grew up to have a son named Jesse; *his* son was David and that, you see, makes Ruth the great-grandmother of King David, the best-loved of all the kings who ever ruled over the Jewish people.

You will find the whole story in the book of Ruth.

No. 4. A SOLDIER'S DREAM

" If you ask me," the soldier went on, " it means trouble. We've been thinking we would win sure—and easy. Your dream means that it isn't going to be that way."

They listened that far, then Gideon smiled to himself and he and his orderly crawled away. Back in their own camp, he told his officers what he had heard.

" And don't worry," he said. " We are going to win."

It came out just that way.

You will find the whole story in Judges 7.

No. 5. THE SURPRISED YOUNG MAN

Saul thought Samuel might be able to tell them something about the lost animals. So he went to him and Samuel told him not to worry about them—they were already found. Then he went on to make Saul the guest of honor at a great feast and to tell him that God had chosen him to be king over his people. Probably in all his life Saul was never so much surprised.

You will find the whole story in I Samuel 9.

No. 6. THE BOY WITH FIVE STONES

His younger brother answered him politely, as a younger brother (or any brother) should but he kept right on learning all he could about the champion until finally some one told King Saul about this boy who was asking so many questions and the king said he wanted to see him. They had a talk and the end of

29

it was that, with King Saul's permission, the boy went out armed only with five smooth stones and his sling (which was quite different from what some boys of today call a sling-*shot*) to do battle with the mighty Philistine. One of the things the Bible does not tell but that I would like to know is what Eliab said after the fight was over.

You will find the whole story in I Samuel **17**.

No. 7. THE SPENT ARROWS

The prince asked the boy to come along with him and gather up the arrows he might shoot at a mark. The boy was glad to go. Jonathan shot an arrow. The boy noted where it fell and started to run to get it. While he was going, Jonathan shot another and called to him that this one was beyond him. The boy returned with both and was given the bow too. " Take them back to the city," Jonathan told him. Just the sort of thing the boy had probably done many times before—nothing unusual about it.

He did not know then, perhaps he never found out, that when Jonathan called to him about the arrow beyond him, the words were a signal to David, who was hidden near by. What it meant was, " My father is still angry. It is not safe for you to come back to court."

After the boy was gone, Jonathan and David had another talk and, though they were grown men and soldiers, it seems more than probable that they shed some tears when they said goodbye. Not long after, Jonathan was killed in battle.

You will find the whole story in I Samuel **20**.

No. 8. THE PROPHET'S STORY

" Instead of going to his own flocks, of which he had so many, he took the poor man's one pet lamb and killed it and gave it to his friend to eat."

When King David heard the story, he was very angry, as angry as you would have been in his place. He began telling how he was going to have the man punished and then the prophet looked him straight in the eye and said, " The man who did that wicked thing is *you*."

You will find the whole story in II Samuel **12**.

No. 9.   THE YOUNG KING'S DREAM

Solomon would have liked to be rich and to be secure from his enemies. He might have asked for a long life. But he thought first of his responsibility to his people, and so he asked God for wisdom—to be able to tell good from bad. When God gave him that, you might think it settled everything but of course it didn't. *Knowing* good from bad does not always mean that a person will *do* the good thing and it is sad to learn that Solomon did some things of which he should have been ashamed.

You will find the whole story in I Kings 3.

No. 10.   THE FOOD THAT LASTED

"First," went on the man—(his name was Elijah and he was a prophet)—"first, cook something for me to eat. If you do, I promise you that the food you have left will last until the rains come again and you can buy more."

The woman believed him and did exactly as he said and in some way (the Bible does not tell us how) the food lasted. It was enough for her, and for her little boy, and for the prophet, until the drought was over and another crop was harvested.

You will find the whole story in I Kings 17.

No. 11.   THE LITTLE CLOUD

He cast himself down there and first he prayed for the rain that had been so long withheld. Then he told his servant to go and look toward the sea. The servant went but returned saying he could see nothing: the western sky was cloudless, just as it had been all these many days past.

"Go again," Elijah told him. "Keep on going."

And, at the seventh time, he came back saying he could see a little cloud "like a man's hand."

"We must hurry," Elijah told him. "A great rain is coming."

That proved true indeed, for ere Ahab in his chariot and Elijah running before him could reach the shelter of the city, rain was falling in torrents.

You will find the whole story in I Kings 18.

No. 12. THE PATRIOT

He made up his mind that he must do something. He loved his country and his countrymen, and for those living in what had once been their capital city to be poor and in constant danger from enemies while he himself was rich, safe and living an easy life—that, he felt, was not right. He had money, friends, ability. If he were there, on the ground, he believed he could help them. So he asked the king if he might go and the king said yes.

You will find the whole story in Nehemiah 1 and 2.

No. 13. THE MAN WHO TRIED TO RUN
AWAY FROM GOD

He ran away—took ship for a distant land. Then a great storm came, sent by God he felt sure to punish him or else to make him obey. He did obey at last and, in doing so, he learned two very important things about God: first, that God is everywhere and, second, that he loves all people, " foreigners " as well as ourselves.

You will find the whole story in the book of Jonah.

No. 14. THE PRAYER JESUS GAVE

Jesus talked to them about praying. They must never, he said, pray to " show off." They must never imagine that there was some special value in thoughtlessly saying the same prayer over and over—ten times, a hundred times, a thousand times. What counts most in a prayer is—do you really mean it. They must not suppose that God needed to be " teased." Then he gave them a sort of sample prayer. Can you repeat it?

You will find the whole story in Matthew 6.

No. 15. THE MESSAGE FROM PRISON

" Jesus will know," he seems to have thought, " and he will give me an honest answer." So he sent two friends who came to Jesus and asked John's question. Jesus did not say, as you might expect, " Yes—I am the man." Instead, for a while he kept John's friends near him to let them see what he was doing. Then

32

he said to them, " Go back to John and tell him what you have seen and heard." When John knows that, he seems to have thought, he will be able to answer his own question.

You will find the whole story in Matthew 11.

No. 16. THE BLIND MAN

Jesus' enemies tried to make trouble for the man who had been cured. They asked him just how he had been healed and what he thought about Jesus. They sent for his parents and asked *them* questions. Was this really their son? And had he been blind? Yes, his parents said, he had even been born blind. They went back to the man himself. They tried to mix him up, to confuse him, to make him believe that Jesus was not a good man. But in all this they failed, because one thing he *knew*— that he had been blind and that now he could see.

You will find the whole story in John 9.

No. 17. THE BOY WHO LEFT HOME

He woke up. " I'm a failure," he said, " and a wicked failure: but one person in this world still cares for me and I am going back to him. I won't ask to be taken back as a son—I don't deserve that: but our hired men always had enough to eat. I will ask him to take me on as one of them."

He started, and when his father saw him coming he ran to meet him. The boy began telling how sorry he was but his father never let him finish. He began shouting orders to the servants: bring food—clothing—new shoes—everything! My lost boy is home again.

You will find the whole story in Luke 15.

No. 18. THE BROTHER WHO WAS NOT GLAD

It is hard to believe but—he was not glad. Instead of rushing in to welcome the brother whom he had not seen for so long, he sat down to sulk: " Why all this great fuss about my brother? When did anybody ever do anything for *me?* " Finally his father had to go out and talk to him. What Jesus meant to teach by his story was, I think, this: it is a bad thing to be always thinking of " good times," of the fun you can have going places and spending money. But not to love one's brother—that is even worse.

You will find the whole story in Luke 15.

No. 19.   THE WEDDING OF THE KING'S SON

Here was the splendid dinner and no one to eat it! So he told his servants to go out into the streets and gather in every one they could find—that banquet was going to be eaten by some one. You can imagine the happiness of the people who had never dreamed they would sit down at a king's table and who now were invited to come in.

I think that what Jesus meant to teach was this: God has provided for us a feast of good things. We may refuse it. (A boy or girl, for instance, may refuse to go to school.) But, if we do, we will suffer for it and the feast will be given to some one else, who better appreciates it.

You will find the whole story in Matthew 22: 1–10.

No. 20.   THE TWO HOUSES

There came a storm, a terrible storm, worse probably than any you ever saw. Wind, rain and then a flood swept about the two houses and beat upon them. Finally the clouds rolled away, the sun came out again and the house built upon the good foundation stood unharmed. There it was, right where it had always been. But the other house was gone. It had fallen and " great was the fall of it."

Perhaps what Jesus wanted to teach was that any one is foolish who tries to build a life on such things as position, or money, or even brains but if he builds it on —— Well, what do *you* think he should build it on?

You will find the whole story in Matthew 7.

No. 21.   LONG AND SHORT TIME WORKERS

They got a surprise. Those who had begun their work at five
34

were paid for a full day's work and the same for the men who had begun work at three, at twelve and at nine. " Well," the first men must have thought, " at that rate we will certainly get more." But they didn't: they got only what had been agreed upon. It seemed to them unfair and they complained. " Why, these men," they said, " have worked only an hour. We have worked all day. Yet the wages we are getting are just the same." " But aren't you getting every cent I promised? " the owner asked them. " And isn't it my own money? Can't I do as I please with it? "

Some people say Jesus meant to teach that, if a man is willing to work, " society " ought to give him a job and pay him a " living wage." Other people have said, " Yes, but what about a man's doing what he pleases with his own money? " It gives us something to think about.

You will find the whole story in Matthew 20.

No. 22. WEEDS AND WHEAT

He told them no. If they tried to do that, a lot of the wheat would be pulled up too. Better let them grow on together. Then, when the wheat was ripe, both could be harvested, the wheat to be put to good use, the weeds to be burned up.

We think sometimes that this world would be better and certainly pleasanter, if only good people lived in it. God could of course make it that way and could take all the bad people out of it, if he wanted to. But to him it does not seem the best way. For the present, we must live with some people who are not good but one day there will be a separation: good people will live with good people and bad people (though they probably will not want to do it) will have to go with bad people.

You will find the whole story in Matthew 13.

No. 23. THE MAN WHO WAS GOING TO ENJOY HIMSELF

That very night he died. Nor was that the worst of it. All his life he seems to have thought about nothing but bigger and better crops. He had never made friends and now no one spoke of how much he would be missed. He had no "treasure in heaven." He was not "rich toward God." The end found him with nothing but things—which he must go away and leave. No wonder this is usually called the story of "The Rich Fool." You see, he had the notion that *things* bring happiness, which is about the most foolish idea that any one can have and leads always to sorrow.

You will find the whole story in Luke 12.

No. 24. FATHER AND SONS

The second son was interrupted, or perhaps he was just lazy, or perhaps he had never intended to do any work—Jesus did not say. Anyway, all day long he never went near the vineyard.

Now, of course, neither boy did *just* the right thing. But Jesus' teaching was that the older one did better. To *do* right is certainly better than to make right promises and break them.

You will find the whole story in Matthew 21.

No. 25. THE MAN WHO WAS UNFORGIVING

The rest is almost unbelievable. The man went out and found a friend to whom he had once loaned twenty dollars. "I want back that money of mine," he said. "I cannot pay it back now," his friend told him. "Give me a little time and I will pay back every cent of it." "I want it now—this minute," he answered. And, when his poor friend could not pay it, he had him put into jail. What happened next you will perhaps imagine. The king heard about it and was very angry. He even tried to correct it but I don't believe he succeeded.

Jesus meant, I think, to teach something like this: Before you tell any one, ever, "I won't forgive you," think about yourself. Did *you* ever need to be forgiven? If you think about it honestly, you may find you have done something, some time, that was far worse than your friend did.

You will find the whole story in Matthew 18.

No. 26. THE MAN WHO WAS SLEEPY

The man never stopped a minute but kept right on telling his troubles, until finally his neighbor said to himself:

" I may as well get up and find something for him. If I don't, he will keep me awake till morning with all this racket."

So he climbed out of bed and gave the man everything he wanted.

I think what Jesus meant to teach by his story was something like this: " Do you think God is like that? That you must beg of him the things that are good for you? If you do, you are greatly mistaken. How about you yourselves—you who are fathers and mothers? When your children come to you, do they have to tease and tease for what they need? Of course not. You love to give them good things. Well, it is the same way with God—only more so."

You will find the whole story in Luke 11.

No. 27. THE MAN WHO CLIMBED A TREE

All he wanted was a glimpse but, when Jesus came by and saw him, he greatly surprised him by calling him by name and saying, " Come down quickly for I must stay at your house today." Even more delighted than he was surprised, Zacchaeus hurried down. Later he gave a feast for Jesus, they became friends and Zacchaeus became a good man.

You will find the whole story in Luke 19.

No. 28. THE MAN IN THE COURTYARD

A girl said to him, " You were with Jesus." He said, " I was not." Another girl said the same thing. Again he denied it—he even swore about it. Then he heard a sound which reminded him of Jesus' warning. Why, here he was doing exactly what he had solemnly promised that he would never do! You can imagine how he felt. And the Bible says that he went out and wept bitterly.

You will find the whole story in Matthew 26.

No. 29. A FOOT-RACE

They had thought every dreadful thing that could happen had happened but she was come to tell them of one more. Jesus' body, she said, had been taken from the tomb where they had laid it. They started at a run to find out and John (probably because he was younger) outran Peter and came to the tomb first. He did not go in but, when Peter came, he went in. They looked about them. What they saw did not seem like the work of grave robbers: and into their minds came the first glimmerings of the wonderful thing of which we are told each Easter morning.

You will find the whole story in John 20.

No. 30. THE MAN WHO WAS PUZZLED

" Do you understand what you are reading? " the man asked. (His name was Philip.)

No, he answered, he did not: and then (probably seeing that Philip was a Jew, who naturally would know more about a Jewish book than he himself) he asked him to get up into the chariot and ride with him. When he did, Philip began telling him the story of Jesus and the man listened and became deeply interested. Finally he asked if he himself might not become one of Jesus' followers and Philip told him he surely might, if he really wished to. After he had been baptized, Philip went away to tell others the same story and the man continued his journey, with the good news of Jesus in his heart.

You will find the whole story in Acts 8.

No. 31. PETER'S DREAM

The visitors were Roman soldiers, sent by their captain, Cornelius, who had heard about Peter and was anxious to hear him preach. Peter listened. He had been told that Cornelius was a good man and it seemed to him that the coming of these soldiers might have something to do with the dream he had just had. When he had heard all they had to tell him, he went with them (though he had been brought up to think it was wrong for him to visit any " foreigner ") and he preached in Cornelius's house. Just think! If he and Paul had not come to believe as they did, our own ancestors (who of course were " foreigners " to them) might never have become Christians.

You will find the whole story in Acts 10.

No. 32. A GIRL NAMED RHODA

She listened and then came running back to them to say that Peter was outside. They told her she must be mistaken. Had she forgotten? Peter was in prison. Certainly, she told them, she knew that as well as they did but he was outside now. She had heard his voice and recognized it. Meanwhile the knocking was keeping right on. At last some one answered the door and found she was right. It *was* Peter and, while they sat wondering at the answer to the prayer they had just been offering, he told them of the marvellous way in which he had been delivered from prison.

You will find the whole story in Acts 12.

No. 33. THE PERSECUTOR

Years later Saul told about it in a speech that he made before a king. " At midday," he said, " I saw in the way a light from heaven and heard a voice saying, ' Saul, Saul, why persecutest thou me? ' "

That was startling enough but it was by no means as important as what followed, for from that day Saul was a changed man—he even changed his name and was called Paul. He became a faithful follower of Jesus and, in all the world of his time, no other man went into so many countries telling about him.

You will find the whole story in Acts 26.

No. 34. THE SHRINE MAKER

He gathered a mob, most of whom had no notion what it was all about, and the mob raised an uproar and behaved foolishly—as most mobs do. They could not find Paul (and his friends would not let him go to them) but they caught two of his friends, threatened them, dragged them into the great, open theatre and for about two hours kept shouting, over and over, " Great is Diana of the Ephesians! " It was all perfectly silly and nothing came of it, really, excepting that Demetrius and his friends were roundly scolded by the authorities.

You will find the whole story in Acts 19.

No. 35. THE SHIPWRECK

The man was Paul, whom his enemies had had arrested and who was now on his way to Rome to have his case come before a higher court—that of the Emperor himself. He had warned them that the voyage would be dangerous but he now stood up to tell them not to worry. The ship, he said, would indeed be lost but their lives, every one of them, would be saved. Then he reminded them that it was now many days they had been on watch without eating anything and, taking food, he blessed it and gave it to them. At daybreak they could see they were near some island and they ran the boat close enough to shore so that all, some of them on planks and pieces of wreckage, were able, just as Paul had promised, to reach land in safety.

You will find the whole story in Acts 27.

"HONEST SERVING MEN" QUIZZES

The "What" Questions

No. 1.   WHAT'S WHAT IN THE *PROVERBS?*

1.   What "exalteth a nation"?
2.   "Where there is no vision, the people . . ." What?
3.   "A wise son maketh . . ."
4.   "A good name is rather to be chosen than . . ."
5.   "Whoso findeth a wife findeth . . ."
6.   "In the multitude of counsellors there is . . ."
7.   "A fair woman that is without discretion . . ." (The present generation might say, "A woman that is beautiful but dumb.") ". . . is like . . ." What?
8.   What is as a shining light "that shineth more and more unto the perfect day"?
9.   "Pride goeth before . . ."
10.   Four things, declares the compiler of the proverbs, are "too wonderful" for him. What are they?

No. 2.   WHAT'S WHAT IN THE *PSALMS?*

1.   A good man, the Psalms tell us, is "like a tree planted by the rivers of water . . . The ungodly are not so but are like . . ." What?
2.   "Let the words of my mouth and the meditations of my heart be . . ."
3.   "Thy rod and thy staff . . ." Do what?
4.   "I have been young, and now am old; yet have I not seen . . ."
5.   "Thou crownest the year with . . ."
6.   "So teach us to number our days that we may . . ."
7.   "As for man, his days are as . . ."
8.   "I said in my haste . . ."

[Answers on page 58]   **41**

9. " Precious in the sight of the Lord is . . ."
10. " Behold how good and pleasant it is for brethren to . . ."

No. 3.   WHAT'S WHAT IN *THE PROPHETS?*

1. " They that wait upon the Lord shall . . ." Do what?
2. " How beautiful upon the mountains are . . ."
3. " We all do fade as . . ."
4. " And they that be wise shall shine as . . . and they that turn many to righteousness as . . ." What?
5. " They have sown the wind and they shall reap . . ."
6. " Your old men shall . . . , your young men shall . . ." What?
7. " What doth God require of thee . . ."
8. " The Lord is in his holy temple; let all the earth . . ." Do what?
9. " Not by might nor by power but by . . ."
10. " But unto you that fear my name shall the Sun of righteousness arise with . . ."

No. 4.   WHAT'S WHAT IN *ECCLESIASTES* AND THE *SONG OF SOLOMON?*

1. " He that increaseth knowledge increaseth . . ." What?
2. " The sleep of the laboring man is . . ."
3. " In the day of prosperity be joyful but in the day of adversity . . ." Do what?
4. " God hath made man upright but they have sought out . . ."
5. " A living dog is better than . . ."
6. " Whatsoever thy hand findeth to do, do it with . . ."
7. " Rejoice, O young man, in thy youth; and let thy heart cheer thee in the days of thy youth . . . but know . . ." What?
8. " Much study is . . ."
9. " Love is as strong as . . . , jealousy is cruel as . . ." What?
10. " Many waters cannot quench . . . neither can the floods drown it."

     [Answers on page 59]

No. 5. WHAT'S WHAT IN *THE GOSPELS?*

1. " Be ye therefore wise as . . . and harmless as . . ."
What?

2. " The tree is known by . . ."

3. " Thou art Peter and upon this rock I will build . . ."

4. " Blind guides which strain at a . . . and swallow
a . . ." What?

5. " Wheresoever the . . . is, there will the . . . be gathered
together."

6. " Woe unto you when all men shall . . ." Do what?

7. A man once came to Jesus, saying, " Master, speak to my
brother, that he divide the inheritance with me." What did
Jesus answer?

8. " Neither do I condemn thee; go and . . ." Do what?

9. " In my father's house are . . ."

10. What was written over the cross upon which Jesus was
crucified?

The " Why " Questions

" Come now, let us reason together," said one of the prophets
and that is exactly what much of the Bible is—reasoning. In
particular you will find this true of some of these " Why " Questions and you should remember that the answer given is seldom
the full answer and sometimes only one of several right answers.
Just as you might give a dozen good answers to the question,
" Why do you love your mother? " so here more than one correct
answer is often possible and a correct answer might well take a
page (or more) instead of only a sentence.

No. 1. OLD TESTAMENT

1. You have probably heard a confused mixture of sounds
called a " Babel." Why?

2. You may have heard some hunter called a " Nimrod."
Why should he be given that name?

3. You have read about how, a runaway from home, Jacob
lay down in a lonely place with a stone for his pillow and

[Answers on pages 59–60]   **43**

dreamed about a ladder reaching to heaven. But why was he a runaway?

4. Why did Joseph's brethren hate him?

5. You have heard about Moses in the bullrushes. Why did his mother put him there? Why didn't she just keep him at home?

6. When Moses was commanded to lead his people out of slavery, he seems to have doubted whether he was the right man for it and to have argued with God about it. Why did he doubt himself?

7. When Samuel was a little boy, he once went to Eli the priest, who had been like a father to him, and told him that great trouble was going to come upon him. Why did he do it?

8. When Saul first became king, some were against him. Then, suddenly, he was immensely popular. Why?

9. After Solomon's reign of great prosperity, the kingdom was split in two. Why?

10. You have heard the story of Daniel in the lions' den. Why was he placed there?

No. 2.   FROM JESUS' LIFE

1. Why did Joseph and Mary, while Jesus was still a baby, take him into Egypt?

2. When, as a twelve-year-old boy, Jesus was taken up to Jerusalem, why did he remain behind?

3. Jesus often condemned the " scribes and Pharisees." Why?

4. Why did not the people of Jesus' home-town become his followers?

5. Jesus scandalized some of the people of his time by eating with " publicans and sinners." Why did he do it?

6. There is in the gospel of Luke a sad story about a young man of good character, who really wanted to be a follower of Jesus but finally " went away grieved." Why?

7. Why did Nicodemus come to talk with Jesus?

8. Why did Jesus weep over Jerusalem?

9. Why did Judas betray Jesus?

44   [Answers on pages 60–61]

10. Pilate finally condemned Jesus to death but, before that, he tried to save him. Why?

No. 3. BEATITUDE " WHY'S "

1. " Blessed are the poor in spirit . . ." Why?
2. " Blessed are they that mourn . . ."
3. " Blessed are the meek . . ."
4. " Blessed are they which do hunger and thirst after righteousness . . ."
5. " Blessed are the merciful . . ."
6. " Blessed are the pure in heart . . ."
7. " Blessed are the peacemakers . . ."
8. " Blessed are they which are persecuted for righteousness' sake . . ."
9. " Blessed are ye, when men shall revile you, and persecute you, and shall say all manner of evil against you falsely, for my sake. Rejoice and be exceeding glad . . ."
10. " Blessed are they that do his commandments . . ."

No. 4. SAYINGS OF JESUS

1. " Let your light so shine before men that . . ."
2. " Love your enemies, bless them that curse you, do good to them that hate you, and pray for them that despitefully use you and persecute you." Why?
3. " Pray to thy Father which is in secret . . ."
4. " Lay up for yourselves treasures in heaven, where neither moth nor dust doth corrupt, and where thieves do not break through and steal . . ."
5. " No man can serve two masters . . ."
6. " Take no thought saying, What shall we eat? or What shall we drink? or Wherewithal shall we be clothed? " (Don't worry.) Why?
7. " Ask . . . seek . . . knock . . ." Why?
8. On the night that he was betrayed, Jesus said to his closest friends, " Watch and pray . . ."
9. Jesus once said, " I am come that . . ." and went on to tell why.

[Answers on pages 61–62]   45

10. In his last talk with his closest friends, Jesus told them, " Let not your hearts be troubled." Why?

No. 5. FROM ACTS

1. Why did the Apostles, in a meeting described in the first chapter of Acts, hold a sort of election?

2. When Peter and John were " straightly threatened " by the council, why did they refuse to heed the warning?

3. Why did Gamaliel advise that Peter and John should be allowed to continue preaching?

4. Why did Paul set out from Jerusalem to go to Damascus?

5. Until Barnabas went bond for him, the church at Jerusalem refused to accept Paul. Why?

6. After Herod had " killed James the brother of John with the sword," he arrested Peter also. Why?

7. In Lystra, Paul and Barnabas were taken for gods and the local priests tried to offer a sacrifice to them. Why?

8. Shortly afterward, in the same city, Paul was stoned. Why?

9. Why were Paul and Silas imprisoned in Philippi?

10. Why did Paul make his last journey to Jerusalem, when (Acts 20, 23) he knew it to be very dangerous?

The " When " Questions

If some one were to ask you, " When was America discovered? " you would answer at once, " Why, in 1492." And, if then you were asked, " A. D. or B. C.? " you would laugh and say, " Why, A. D. of course." But in the Bible we find no such dates. When the Bible was written, people did not reckon time in that way and so " When " Questions about the Bible (excepting as we read it in connection with other books) are not answered by giving dates but by —— Well, try two or three and you will see how they go.

No. 1

1. The wonderful first chapter of Genesis, the book of beginnings, opens with the words, " In the beginning God . . ."

 [Answers on pages 62–63]

(No one can go farther back than that.) Then it goes on with the story of how the heavens and the earth were made, telling it as if God were a great workman, completing one thing one day, another the next and so on. In this story when did God make man? On what day of the week?

2. When did he make the sun, moon and stars?

3. The story goes on to say that God completed his work, saw that everything he had made was good and rested—when?

4. When (at what age) was Abraham commanded to leave the country that had always been his home and go into a new land that some day would belong to his descendants?

5. You have heard of Jacob's wrestling with an angel. When (at what time of his life) did it happen?

6. When was Joseph made prime minister of Egypt? What event led to it?

7. Joseph's brothers made three journeys into Egypt. When (on which journey) did they learn who was the " great man " who had been giving them food?

8. When did the oppression of the Israelites in Egypt begin?

9. When (during what Judgeship) did the Israelites decide that they wanted to have a king to rule over them?

10. When did his call come to the prophet Isaiah?

No. 2

1. When was Jesus born?
2. When did he first see Jerusalem?
3. When did Jesus begin his ministry?
4. When (at what hour) did Nicodemus come to visit Jesus?
5. When (what day of the week) was Jesus crucified?
6. When (what day of the week) did he rise from the dead?
7. When, after Jesus' death, was the good news of his teaching first carried beyond the borders of Palestine?
8. When was the first great missionary journey of the early church undertaken?
9. When was Christianity first brought to Europe?
10. When will the end of the world come?

[Answers on pages 63–64]

The "How" Questions

No. 1. OLD TESTAMENT STORIES

1. How did God create man?
2. When there was a quarrel between the servants of Lot and the servants of Abraham, how was it settled?
3. When Joseph was in prison, two fellow prisoners asked him to interpret their dreams for them. How did he do it?
4. How did Joshua begin his invasion of the Promised Land?
5. How did Samuel come to be a judge over Israel?
6. King Saul's sick mind brought him suffering and often made him dangerous. How was he sometimes soothed?
7. When David was in great danger among the Philistines, at the court of Achish, king of Gath, how did he save himself?
8. The Bible has a fine, exciting story about two spies who were being closely followed but got into a courtyard where a friendly woman saved them from being captured. How did she do it?
9. Two women once came to King Solomon, each claiming the same baby. How did he find out which one was the real mother?
10. When Daniel's enemies wanted to get him into trouble, how did they do it?

No. 2. THE PSALMS

Some of the most famous and beautiful figures of speech in all literature are found in the Psalms.

1. A sublime passage in one of the Psalms describes the sun: "Which is as a bridegroom coming out of his chamber and rejoiceth . . ." How?
2. "As . . . so panteth my soul after thee, O God." How?
3. "For all our days are passed away in thy wrath; we spend our years . . ."
4. "O worship the Lord . . . fear before him all the earth."
5. "He cometh to judge the earth; he shall judge the world . . ."
6. We are told that God has removed the sins of those forgiven—how far?

[Answers on pages 64–65]

7. ". . . so the Lord pitieth them that fear him."

8. "How" (this is Moffatt's translation) "can a young man keep life clean?"

9. "He that goeth forth and weepeth, bearing precious seed, shall doubtless come again . . ."

10. "O give thanks unto the Lord, for he is good; for his mercy endureth . . ." (In one Psalm the answering word is repeated twenty-six times.)

No. 3.   THE GOSPELS

1. How did the Wise Men know of the coming birth of Jesus?

2. How was John the Baptist dressed?

3. How successful was John the Baptist's preaching?

4. Once upon a time Jesus was preaching inside a house. Around it the crowd was so dense that no one could get in but some men wanted to bring a sick friend to him so that he could be healed. How did they manage it?

5. When John the Baptist was in prison, he sent some of his friends to Jesus to ask, "Art thou he that should come or do we look for another?" How did Jesus answer them?

6. A Roman officer once besought Jesus to cure his servant but, not wishing to trouble him, he suggested that he cure him —how?

7. We are told that the people were astonished at Jesus' teaching, because he taught them—how?

8. Jesus was crucified between two thieves. How did they behave themselves?

9. How did Judas die?

10. How was Thomas finally convinced that Jesus had really risen from the dead?

No. 4.   THE ACTS

1. How did Jesus' followers, in the very beginning, handle their money matters?

2. How did Ananias try to gain credit that he did not deserve?

[Answers on pages 65–66]   **49**

3. How did Stephen die?

4. How did the chief treasurer of Candace, Queen of Ethiopia, come to learn about Jesus?

5. One time, when Paul was in Damascus and the authorities were watching every gate hoping to arrest him, friends contrived his escape—how?

6. How did Paul and his friends come to decide to carry the good news about Jesus to Europe?

7. How did it happen that Paul, who had taken every precaution to avoid trouble, was arrested while in Jerusalem?

8. When arrested in Jerusalem, Paul was about to be whipped but escaped it—how?

9. Paul had long wanted to go to Rome to preach. How did he finally get there?

10. In Rome, Paul was given considerate treatment and lived " in his own hired house." How long?

The " Where " Questions

No. 1. ABOUT MOSES

1. Where was he born?

2. Where did he receive his formal education?

3. Where did he go as a fugitive, to escape Pharaoh?

4. Under orders from Jehovah he later went—where?

5. In leading his people out of slavery, what sea did he cross?

6. Where was he while transforming his people from a servile race to a nation capable of aggressive action?

7. To what land did he finally lead his people?

8. Where did he receive the law often called by his name?

9. Where did he die?

10. In the New Testament his name is associated with what mountain?

No. 2. ABOUT DAVID

1. Where did he spend his boyhood?

2. His most spectacular fight was with a giant who came from—where?

[Answers on pages 66–67]

3. When he and his men were leading a sort of Robin Hood life, frequently hunted by King Saul, where did he make head-quarters?

4. Where did he get his following?

5. Where at this time did he place his parents, so that they might be out of danger?

6. When closely pursued by Saul, where did he himself at last seek refuge?

7. Where was he anointed—for the second time?

8. Where did he later make his capital?

9. Where did he wish to build a temple to Jehovah?

10. Where was the final, decisive battle fought between his own forces and those of his rebellious son Absalom?

No. 3.   ABOUT JESUS

1. Where was he born?

2. Where did the wise men come from, they who brought him gifts?

3. Where was he when the aged Simeon saw in him, " A light to lighten the Gentiles and the glory of thy people Israel " ?

4. Where did Joseph and Mary take him to escape King Herod?

5. Where did he spend his boyhood?

6. Did he ever make his home in any other place?

7. Where did he do most of his teaching?

8. Where else did he teach and preach?

9. Where was he when taken by the mob?

10. Where was he crucified?

No. 4.   ABOUT PAUL

1. Where was he reared?   (He speaks of it as " no mean city.")

2. Where did he complete his education?

3. Where was he going, when he had the experience which resulted in his becoming a Christian?

4. From what city did he (and Barnabas) set forth upon the first of his missionary journeys?

[Answers on page 67]   51

5. Where did they go first?

6. Where did he first preach the gospel in Europe?

7. Where did he find the altar " To the Unknown God," which gave him the text for one of his greatest sermons?

8. Where was he imprisoned for two years?

9. Where was he shipwrecked?

10. Where do we find him at the conclusion of the book of Acts?

No. 5. WHERE DO YOU FIND . . . ?

We sometimes sing, " Thy word is like an armory " and the comparison is a good one, for an armory should not only be well equipped—which the Bible is—one should be able to turn instantly to anything in it that he wishes to use.

1. Where do you find the stories of the Creation, the Flood and the Tower of Babel?

2. Where do you find the Ten Commandments?

3. One of the greatest choruses in Haydn's *Creation* is a paraphrase of the words, " The heavens declare the glory of God," etc. Where do you find them?

4. Where do you find the book of Hezekiah?

5. Where do you find the first book of Maccabees?

6. The acts of David are written in the book of the Prophet Nathan. Is this true or false?

7. Where do you find the Sermon on the Mount?

8. Where do you find the Lord's Prayer?

9. Where do you find the story of the resurrection?

10. Where do you find the Bible's fullest description of Heaven?

The " Who " Questions

No. 1. WHO'S WHO IN GENESIS?

Name, if you can, the persons described.

1. Tennyson mentions a " gardener " and his wife who " smile at the claims of long descent."

2. Better known for a crime, it is also recorded of him that he built the first city.

52   [Answers on pages 67–68]

3. He was the first of all metal workers.

4. He received God's promise in the rainbow.

5. His mother was told, before his birth, " His hand shall be against every man and every man's hand against him."

6. Her lover served for her seven years and then, being deceived and defrauded, served seven years more.

7. His sons and grandsons gave their names to the twelve tribes of Israel.

8. " A cunning hunter, a man of the field," he is best known for having sold his birthright for a mess of pottage.

9. Himself a shrewd and not always scrupulous bargainer, he was worsted in a " deal " made with his son-in-law.

10. The hero of one of the best and earliest of the world's short stories, his life has been retold in our day (in four volumes) by one of the greatest of living novelists.

No. 2. WHO'S WHO IN JOSHUA AND JUDGES?

Name, if you can, the persons described.

1. When the great leader of the exodus was laid to rest, he took over and led the invasion of Palestine.

2. In applying for a difficult and dangerous military task, he declared that, at eighty-five, he was now as strong as when, returning from a youthful scouting expedition, he had favored the immediate invasion of the Promised Land.

3. A "mother in Israel," she is the only woman listed as having been a judge of her people.

4. " One of the most ancient and magnificent remains of Hebrew literature " praises her for what, to our generation, seems a cold-blooded and treacherous murder.

5. An enemy of Israel, it is said of him that the stars in their courses fought against him.

6. The ranking military commander of his people, he refused to lead his troops into battle unless a certain woman would go with him.

7. Pictured as a man of tremendous strength and dauntless courage, he was never a real leader among his people, was the victim of his own follies and extravagances and died (howbeit heroically) as a prisoner of his enemies.

[Answers on pages 68–69]   53

8.   He won a great victory for his people but today might be numbered with the minor judges of Israel, save for one thing—a rash vow which he made and kept.

9.   Leading a handful of amazingly armed shock troops, he won a brilliant victory in a night attack upon an enemy by whom he was vastly outnumbered.

10.   Bribed by the leaders of her own people, she betrayed her lover into their hands—a man whom they regarded as the most dangerous of their enemies.

No. 3.   WHO'S WHO IN SAMUEL?

Name, if you can, the persons described.

1.   She took her son to the temple and there " lent him to the Lord " but each year went to see him, bringing him a little coat.

2.   He died on learning that the ark of God, of which he was the official custodian, had been taken in battle by the Philistines.

3.   A child, sleeping alone in the sanctuary, he was summoned to a hard task—that of foretelling disaster to the old man who all his life had been to him like a kind father.

4.   He went out seeking some strayed farm animals and returned the anointed king of his people.

5.   A king's son and the hero of his people, he narrowly escaped execution as a result of eating a little honey.

6.   Once a king's commanding general, he decided, on his master's death, to change sides. The result was that he was murdered by one who saw in him a possible rival.

7.   A brave and loyal soldier, he was treacherously slain, because a king coveted his wife.

8.   A strikingly handsome man of marked ability, he rose in rebellion against his own father and almost succeeded in dethroning him.

9.   A shrewd planner of treason for the above prince, it was said of him that " he counselled . . . as if a man had inquired at the oracle of God." When his counsels were rejected, he died a suicide.

10.   He is described as " the sweet psalmist of Israel."

54
[Answers on page 69]

No. 4. WHO'S WHO AMONG THE PROPHETS?

Name, if you can, the persons described.

1. In Sargent's famous mural of The Prophets, his is the central figure.

2. When a powerful king, his personal friend, committed a great sin, he had the courage to go to him and reprove him for it.

3. In the reaction which followed his greatest victory over heathen rivals, he fled from a woman's threat and " requested for himself that he might die."

4. He once angered a foreign dignitary by telling him (through a servant) how he might be healed of a loathsome disease—instead of going through the expected incantation.

5. More clearly than any other voice does his foretell for us the coming of the Christ.

6. His prophecies were so resented that, by a king's order, he was thrown into a miry dungeon where he might have died but for a slave's intervention on his behalf.

7. The one thing that every one knows about him is that he was once cast into a den of lions.

8. (Put the word in its feminine form.) Luke describes her as a woman of great age, who " served God with fastings and prayers night and day," and who recognized the infant Christ, when he was brought to the temple.

9. We do not commonly think of him as belonging to the prophetic order, yet Jesus said of him that he was " a prophet and more than a prophet."

10. His name is mentioned only twice in the Bible: once when he foretells a famine, once when as a sign he binds his own hands and feet with another man's girdle.

No. 5. WHO'S WHO IN THE GOSPELS?

Name, if you can, the persons described.

1. A king because of whose anger Joseph took the young child and his mother and with them fled into Egypt.

2. A " just and devout man waiting for the consolation of

[Answers on page 69]

Israel," who felt that the climax of his life was reached when he saw and recognized the Christ child.

3. A tax gatherer, whom Jesus summoned from his despised calling to become one of his closest associates.

4. Devoted to Jesus to the point of being willing to die for him, he has yet come to be known as " the doubter."

5. Next to Peter probably the best known of all the apostles —though the least worthy.

6. Two brothers, for whom their mother once unwisely asked that, when the Master came into his kingdom, they might sit, the one on his right hand, the other on his left.

7. Two sisters, living with their brother Lazarus in Bethany, each—in her own way—devoted to the Master.

8. A member of the Sanhedrin, he was so much impressed by the teaching of Jesus that he sought him out for a personal interview.

9. The Roman governor whose authority it was necessary to have before sentence of death could be passed upon Jesus.

10. A rich man who, after the crucifixion, asked the authorities for the body of Jesus, that he might give it fitting burial.

No. 6. WHO'S WHO IN THE ACTS?

Name, if you can, the persons described.

1. His name occurs twice in the Bible: once in the dedication to the Gospel of Luke, once in the dedication to the book of Acts. He may have been a Roman official but this is not certain.

2. He was chosen by the apostles to take the place in their number left vacant by the traitor Judas. After that we hear nothing of him.

3. A well-educated, professional man, he served Paul as his personal physician and later became his biographer.

4. When Peter and John were brought before the Sanhedrin, his advice was that they be released for a time, arguing that, if they were preaching folly, no harm would come of it; if they were preaching the truth, the Sanhedrin might find itself " fighting against God."

5. Elected to what appeared merely an administrative posi-

 [Answers on pages 69–70]

tion, he proved himself so convincing a speaker that he won the implacable enmity of the religious " stand-patters " and became the first Christian martyr.

6. Wishing for the glory of putting his money into the common fund of the church but unwilling to part with *all* of it, he took the hazardous course of lying to the apostle Peter. His name has come to be synonymous with " liar."

7. His appearance must have been strikingly impressive for, on one of his missionary journeys with Paul, the local priests saw in him an incarnation of Jupiter and tried to offer a formal sacrifice.

8. A Roman officer on duty in Jerusalem, he ordered a prisoner to be scourged and then thought better of it—on learning that he was a Roman citizen.

9. A venial Roman governor, he kept Paul long in prison (though he seems to have rather liked him), hoping that he might be bribed to release him.

10. His case is one of history's little ironies. A king, a man of education too and of much influence in the Roman Empire, he would today be utterly forgotten had he not one day listened to a speech made by a certain prisoner awaiting trial.

[Answers on page 70]   57

ANSWERS

Section II

"HONEST SERVING MEN" QUIZZES

The "What" Questions

No. 1.   WHAT'S WHAT IN THE *PROVERBS?*

Oct. 31/93

1. Righteousness. Prov. 14: 34.
2. ". . . perish." Prov. 29: 18.
3. ". . . a glad father." Prov. 10: 1.
4. ". . . great riches." Prov. 22: 1.
5. ". . . a good thing." Prov. 18: 22.
6. ". . . safety." Prov. 11: 14.
7. "A jewel of gold in a swine's snout." Prov. 11: 22.
8. "The path of the just." Prov. 4: 18.
9. ". . . destruction." Prov. 16: 18.
10.   The way of (1) an eagle in the air (2) a serpent upon the rock (3) a ship in the sea and (4) a man with a maid. Prov. 30: 19.

No. 2.   WHAT'S WHAT IN *THE PSALMS?*

Oct 31/93

1. ". . . the chaff which the wind driveth away." Psl. 1.
2. ". . . acceptable in thy sight, O Lord, my strength and my redeemer." Psl. 19: 14.
3. ". . . they comfort me." Psl. 23.
4. ". . . the righteous forsaken, nor his seed begging bread." Psl. 37: 25.
5. ". . . thy goodness." Psl. 65: 11.
6. ". . . apply our hearts unto wisdom." Psl. 90: 12.
7. ". . . as grass; as a flower of the field, so he flourisheth." Psl. 103: 15.
8. ". . . all men are liars." Psl. 116: 11.
9. ". . . the death of his saints." Psl. 116: 15.
10. ". . . dwell together in unity." Psl. 133: 1.

58

No. 3.   WHAT'S WHAT IN *THE PROPHETS?*

1. ". . . renew their strength." Isa. 40: 31.
2. ". . . the feet of him that bringeth good tidings, that publisheth peace." Isa. 52: 7.
3. ". . . a leaf." Isa. 64: 6.
4. ". . . as the brightness of the firmament . . . as the stars forever and ever." Dan. 12: 3.
5. ". . . the whirlwind." Hosea 8: 7.
6. ". . . dream dreams . . . see visions." Joel 2: 28.
7. ". . . but to do justly, and to love mercy, and to walk humbly with thy God." Micah 6: 8.
8. ". . . keep silence before him." Hab. 2: 20.
9. ". . . my spirit, saith the Lord of Hosts." Zach. 4: 6.
10. ". . . healing in his wings." Malachi 4: 2.

No. 4.   WHAT'S WHAT IN *ECCLESIASTES* AND *THE SONG OF SOLOMON?*

1. ". . . sorrow." Eccl. 1: 18.
2. ". . . sweet." Eccl. 5: 12.
3. ". . . consider." Eccl. 7: 14.
4. ". . . many inventions." Eccl. 7: 29.
5. ". . . a dead lion." Eccl. 9: 4.
6. ". . . thy might." Eccl. 9: 10.
7. ". . . that for all these things God will bring thee into judgment." Eccl. 11: 9.
8. ". . . a weariness of the flesh." Eccl. 12: 12.
9. ". . . death . . . the grave." Song of Sol. 8: 6.
10. ". . . love . . ." Song of Sol. 8: 7.

No. 5.   WHAT'S WHAT IN *THE GOSPELS?*

1. ". . . serpents . . . doves." Matt. 10: 16.
2. ". . . its fruit." Matt. 12: 33.
3. ". . . my church." Matt. 16: 18.
4. ". . . gnat . . . camel." Matt. 23: 24.
5. ". . . carcass . . . eagles . . ." Matt. 24: 28.
6. ". . . speak well of you." Luke 6: 26.

7. " Who made me a judge or a divider over you? . . . Beware of covetousness." Luke 12: 13–15.

8. ". . . sin no more." John 8: 11.

9. ". . . many mansions." John 14: 2.

10. " This is Jesus of Nazareth the King of the Jews." Matt. 27: 37.

The " Why " Questions

No. 1. OLD TESTAMENT

1. The word comes from the story of the Tower of Babel, where we were told the languages of the people were made different, so that they could not understand one another. Gen. 11: 7.

2. In the tenth chapter of Genesis, we read that Nimrod " was a mighty hunter before the Lord."

3. He had fooled his father and cheated his twin brother, who was now very angry at him. No wonder he wanted to get away. Gen. 27.

4. He was his father's " pet." Also, he was perfectly sure that he was smarter than any of his brothers and he took no trouble to keep them from knowing that he thought so. It looks as if Joseph himself were partly to blame.

5. Moses' people were being ruled by the Egyptians, who passed a cruel law that —— Well, what it amounted to was that there were to be no boy babies in Jewish homes.

6. Moses said that he was " slow of speech and of a slow tongue." Ex. 4: 10–14.

7. It had come to him in the night, as an order from God.

8. Because of his swift and successful campaign against the Ammonites, who were besieging Jabesh-Gilead. I Sam. 11.

9. Solomon's son, Rehoboam, foolishly refused to do anything about correcting certain abuses that had sprung up during his father's reign. I Kings 12.

10. He broke a law (a foolish law) made up on purpose to get him into trouble. Dan. 6.

No. 2. FROM JESUS' LIFE

1. To save him from King Herod. Matt. 2.

2. Seemingly he had no thought of being disobedient: he was just so interested in what was going on in the temple that he forgot everything else. Luke 2.

3. Because they were not really loving but made religion a matter of rules and forms.

4. Apparently they could not believe in the greatness of one whom they had seen from childhood, doing every-day duties.

5. " I came," he said, " not to call the righteous but sinners to repentance." Mark 2: 17.

6. Jesus had told him to sell what he had and give it to the poor. That he could not quite bring himself to do, " for he had great possessions." Mark 10: 22.

7. The things that Jesus had done made him realize that Jesus was " a teacher come from God." John 3.

8. He foresaw the troubles that were sure to come upon it: a time when not one stone would be left upon another. Luke 19.

9. For one thing, he was paid money for it. All his reasons we cannot of course know.

10. Jesus' personality had deeply impressed him. Also, he knew perfectly well that Jesus was an innocent man. Luke 23.

No. 3.   BEATITUDE " WHY'S "

1. ". . . for theirs is the kingdom of heaven." Matt. 5: 3.
2. ". . . for they shall be comforted." Matt. 5: 4.
3. ". . . for they shall inherit the earth." Matt. 5: 5.
4. ". . . for they shall be filled." Matt. 5: 6.
5. ". . . for they shall obtain mercy." Matt. 5: 7.
6. ". . . for they shall see God." Matt. 5: 8.
7. ". . . for they shall be called the children of God." Matt. 5: 9.
8. ". . . for theirs is the kingdom of heaven." Matt. 5: 10.
9. ". . . for great is your reward in heaven." Matt. 5: 12.
10. ". . . that they may have right to the tree of life and may enter in through the gates into the city." Revelation 22: 14.

No. 4. SAYINGS OF JESUS

1. ". . . they may see your good works and glorify your Father which is in heaven." Matt. 5: 16.

2. "That ye may be the children of your Father, which is in heaven, for he maketh his sun to rise on the evil and the good, and sendeth his rain on the just and on the unjust." Matt. 5: 44–45.

3. ". . . and thy Father, which seeth in secret, shall reward thee openly." Matt. 6: 6.

4. ". . . for where your treasure is there will your heart be also." Matt. 6: 20–21.

5. ". . . for either he will hate the one and love the other; or else he will hold to the one and despise the other. Ye cannot serve God and mammon." Matt. 6: 24.

6. "For your heavenly Father knoweth that ye have need of all these things." Matt. 6: 32.

7. "For every one that asketh receiveth; and he that seeketh findeth; and to him that knocketh it shall be opened." Matt. 7: 8–9.

8. ". . . lest ye enter into temptation." Mark 14: 38.

9. ". . . that they might have life, and that they might have it more abundantly." John 10: 10.

10. "Ye believe in God, believe also in me." John 14: 1. (The rest of the chapter goes on to explain further.)

No. 5. FROM ACTS

1. To choose a successor for Judas.

2. They said, "whether it be right in the sight of God to hearken unto you more than unto God, judge ye." Acts 4: 19.

3. His argument was: "If this counsel or this work be of men, it will come to naught; but, if it be of God, ye cannot overthrow it." Acts 5.

4. To arrest any Christians whom he might find there. Acts 9.

5. They feared (and naturally) that he might be a spy. Acts 9: 26–27.

6. "Because he saw it pleased the Jews." Acts 12: 2–3.

7. Because of their healing of a lifelong cripple. Acts 14.

8. "Certain Jews from Antioch and Iconium" came to the city and grossly slandered him. Acts 14. (How violently changeable people can be!)

9. Because of the healing of a slave girl, whose "spirit of divination" had been a source of profit to her owners. Acts 16.

10. He went to see old friends and also, and especially, to take a gift from new converts to the mother church at Jerusalem. Acts 24: 17.

The "When" Questions

No. 1

1. The sixth day. Gen. 1: 27.
2. The fourth day. Gen. 1: 14, 19.
3. The seventh day. Gen. 2: 2–3.
4. When he was seventy-five. Gen. 12: 4.
5. When he was returning to his homeland, after his long stay with Laban, and dreaded to meet his brother Esau. Gen. 32.
6. When he was called from prison, to interpret the puzzling dreams of King Pharaoh. Gen. 40–41.
7. On their second journey. Gen. 45.
8. When "there arose a new king over Egypt, who knew not Joseph." Ex. 1: 8–11.
9. During the judgeship of Samuel. I Sam. 8.
10. "In the year that King Uzziah died." Isa. 6.

No. 2

1. In the reign of Augustus Cæsar. Luke 2: 1–2.
2. Not as a boy of twelve (as some may answer) but as a baby. Luke 2: 22.
3. When about thirty years of age. Luke 3: 23.
4. "By night." John 3: 2. Some people think he came then because he did not want to be seen coming. It may have been because Jesus was so busy during the day.
5. On Friday: we call it "Good Friday."
6. On Sunday: the day we celebrate as Easter.

7. When they were scattered "upon the persecution that arose about Stephen." Acts 11: 19.

8. When the church at Antioch solemnly commissioned Paul and Barnabas for the work. Acts 13: 2.

9. When it was preached by Paul and his companions in Macedonia. Acts 16.

10. Jesus' disciples once asked him this question. He told them to be ready for it at any time but "of that day and hour knoweth no man, no, not the angels of heaven but my Father only." Matt. 24: 3, 36.

The "How" Questions

No. 1. OLD TESTAMENT STORIES

1. A correct answer is: "in his own image." Gen. 1: 27. Or "of the dust of the ground." Gen. 2: 7.

2. Abraham said to Lot, "Have it your own way. Choose any part of the land you wish and I will take some other part." Gen. 13.

3. One dream, he said, meant return of the king's favor, the other meant early execution. Gen. 40.

4. He first sent out spies. Then, having crossed the Jordan River, he laid siege to Jericho. Joshua 2 and 6.

5. As a little boy, his mother "lent him to the Lord," and he was brought up in the temple, by Eli the high priest. I Sam. 1.

6. By the playing of a harp. I Sam. 16.

7. By pretending that he was crazy. I Sam. 21: 10–15.

8. She let them down into a well, covered the well's mouth and then spread ground corn over the covering. II Sam. 17.

9. He said, "Why, divide it." Then of course the real mother said, "No! No! I'd rather have you give the baby to the other woman." I Kings 3.

10. They knew he prayed to God every day. So they got the king to pass a law that for thirty days no one should ask anything of any one but *him*. When Daniel paid no attention to the new law but kept right on praying just the same, his enemies had him arrested. Dan. 6.

No. 2.   THE PSALMS

1.   ". . . as a strong man to run a race." Psl. 19: 5.
2.   ". . . the hart panteth after the water brooks . . ."
Psl. 42: 1.
3.   ". . . as a tale that is told." Psl. 90: 9.
4.   ". . . in the beauty of holiness . . ." Psl. 96: 9.
5.   ". . . with righteousness and the people with his truth."
Psl. 96: 13.
6.   " As far as the east is from the west." Psl. 103: 12.
7.   " Like as a father pitieth his children . . ." Psl. 103: 13.
8.   " By keeping to thy word." The authorized version says,
" By taking heed thereto, according to thy word." Psl. 119: 9.
9.   ". . . with rejoicing, bring his sheaves with him." Psl.
126: 6.
10.   ". . . forever." Psl. 136: 1.

No. 3.   THE GOSPELS

1.   The only explanation they gave was, " We have seen his
star in the east and are come to worship him." Matt. 2: 2.
2.   " John had his raiment of camel's hair and a leathern
girdle about his loins." Matt. 3: 4.
3.   " There went out unto him all the land of Judea and they
of Jerusalem." Mark 1: 5.
4.   " They went upon the housetop and let him down through
the tiling." Luke 5: 19.
5.   He kept them with him long enough for them to see for
themselves what he was doing. Then he told them to go back
and tell John what they had seen and heard. Luke 7: 18–23.
6.   " Say in a word and my servant shall be healed." Luke
7: 1–9.
7.   " As one having authority and not as the scribes." Matt.
7: 29.
8.   One reviled him. The other was penitent and Jesus promised him, " Today shalt thou be with me in Paradise." Luke
23: 43.
9.   He hanged himself. Matt. 27: 5.
10.   By the sense of touch. John 20.

No. 4. THE ACTS

1. By a sort of communism, which later they abandoned. It does not appear to have worked very well. Acts 4: 32–34.

2. By claiming he had turned in all his property to the common fund, when really he had turned in only part of it. Acts 5.

3. He was stoned. Acts 7.

4. He was told by a man named Philip, whom he met as he was returning home in his chariot from Jerusalem. Acts 8.

5. At night they let him down from the wall in a basket. Acts 9: 25.

6. Paul had a dream in which a man of Macedonia stood by him and said, " Come over into Macedonia and help us." Acts 16: 9.

7. He was recognized by enemies. They stirred up the people, who mobbed him. Acts 21: 27.

8. By telling the officer that he was a Roman citizen. Acts 22: 25.

9. At the expense of the government—as a prisoner. Acts 25: 12.

10. " Two whole years." Acts 28: 30.

The " Where " Questions

No. 1. ABOUT MOSES

1. In Egypt, probably in the land of Goshen—the territory assigned to the Israelites.

2. In the court of Pharaoh.

3. To the land of Midian.

4. Back to Egypt.

5. The Red Sea.

6. In the deserts of Arabia.

7. In the Land of Canaan—the Promised Land.

8. On Mount Sinai, also called Mount Horeb.

9. On Mount Nebo, also called Mount Pisgah, from which he viewed the Promised Land.

10. The Mount of Transfiguration.

No. 2.   ABOUT DAVID

1. In Bethlehem.
2. Gath.
3. At the Cave of Adullam.
4. We read that "every one that was in distress . . . in debt . . . discontented gathered themselves unto him." Being their leader must have been splendid practice for one who was to be king over a dozen squabbling tribes.
5. In the kingdom of Moab. I Sam. 22: 3.
6. Among the Philistines.
7. At Hebron, by the elders of Israel.
8. At Jerusalem.
9. Also in Jerusalem, upon Mount Moriah.
10. In the wood of Ephraim.

No. 3.   ABOUT JESUS

1. In Bethlehem of Judea.
2. The Bible says nothing more than that they were "from the east."
3. In the temple at Jerusalem—as a baby.
4. To Egypt.
5. In Nazareth.
6. Yes. In Capernaum. Matt. 4: 13.
7. In Galilee.
8. In Judea and Samaria; also in the "coasts of Tyre and Sidon." Matt. 15: 21.
9. In the Garden of Gethsemane.
10. Upon Mount Golgotha, outside the walls of Jerusalem.

No. 4.   ABOUT PAUL

1. In Tarsus.
2. In Jerusalem: "at the feet of Gamaliel."
3. To Damascus.
4. From Antioch.
5. To the island of Cyprus—Barnabas's old home.
6. In Macedonia: Philippi would seem to have been the first city.

7. In Athens.
8. In Caesarea.
9. Upon the island of Melita (Malta).
10. In Rome, in " his own hired house."

No. 5. WHERE DO YOU FIND . . . ?

1. In the early chapters of Genesis.
2. In Exodus 20 and Deuteronomy 5.
3. In Psalm 19.
4. You would be unwise to look for it at all: there is no such book in the Bible.
5. Not in the Bible as commonly printed today. It is one of the books of the Apocrypha.
6. True. This is one of several ancient books (I Chron. 29: 29) which have not come down to our time.
7. Matthew 5, 6 and 7. Much of its substance is also found in Luke and Mark.
8. Matthew 6: 9. Luke 11: 2.
9. In the last chapters of any of the four gospels.
10. In the last chapter of Revelation.

The " Who " Questions

No. 1.   WHO'S WHO IN GENESIS?

1. Adam and Eve.
2. Cain. Gen. 4: 17.
3. Tubal Cain.
4. Noah.
5. Ishmael.
6. Rachel.
7. Jacob.
8. Esau.
9. Laban.
10. Joseph.

No. 2.   WHO'S WHO IN JOSHUA AND JUDGES?

1. Joshua.
2. Caleb.

3. Deborah.
4. Jael.
5. Sisera.   Judg. 5: 20.
6. Barak.   Judg. 4.
7. Samson.
8. Jephthah.
9. Gideon.
10. Delilah.

No. 3.   WHO'S WHO IN SAMUEL?

1. Hannah.
2. Eli.
3. Samuel.
4. Saul.
5. Jonathan.   I Sam. 14: 27.
6. Abner.
7. Uriah.
8. Absolom.
9. Ahithophel.
10. David.

No. 4.   WHO'S WHO AMONG THE PROPHETS?

1. Moses.
2. Nathan.
3. Elijah.
4. Elisha.
5. Isaiah.
6. Jeremiah.
7. Daniel.
8. Anna.
9. John the Baptist.
10. Agabus.

No. 5.   WHO'S WHO IN THE GOSPELS?

1. Herod.
2. Simeon.
3. Matthew (Levi).

4. Thomas.
5. Judas.
6. James and John.
7. Mary and Martha.
8. Nicodemus.
9. Pilate.
10. Joseph of Arimathea.

No. 6. WHO'S WHO IN THE ACTS?

1. Theophilus.
2. Matthias. Acts 1.
3. Luke.
4. Gamaliel.
5. Stephen.
6. Ananias.
7. Barnabas.
8. Claudius Lysias.
9. Felix. Acts 24: 26.
10. Agrippa.

SECTION III

THE BEST OF THE BIBLE

What is the best of the Bible? I have just looked at my mother's and find it has 984 pages. If yours has that many and you could keep only 50, which would you choose?

Not all people of course would pick the same pages but most, I believe, would say that, though there are parts of the Old Testament which they would not part with at any price, the Bible's best pages are those telling about Jesus—the things he did and said:

First some of the ——

No. 1. THINGS THAT JESUS DID

We must always remember that he did *many* more things than those told of him. For instance in John's gospel we read, " Jesus wept." Nowhere do we read, " Jesus smiled." Yet can you imagine him surrounded by little children and not smiling at them? He, who was always talking about joy? Of course he smiled. As to other things:

1. Did Jesus ever earn his living by manual labor?
2. Did Jesus ever read aloud?
3. Jesus was, as one of our hymns says, a " friend of little children." When parents brought their children to him, what did he do?
4. Was Jesus ever sick?
5. Jesus was once asked if it were lawful to pay tribute to Caesar. Did he himself ever pay taxes?
6. Did Jesus ever write anything?
7. Did Jesus ever warn people of dangers and evils that lay ahead?
8. Did Jesus ever sing?
9. Did Jesus ever prepare a meal?
10. Jesus of course did countless things that we cannot do.

Yet Peter once condensed his life into four words that offer a not impossible program for every one of us. What did Peter say?

THINGS JESUS SAID: RECORDED BY MATTHEW

Since these were words spoken by Jesus, they are among the most famous words ever spoken by any one. Can you complete the quotations?

1. " Lay not up for yourselves treasures upon earth, where moth and rust doth corrupt and where thieves break through and steal but . . ."
2. " Judge not . . ." Why?
3. " Ye shall know them by their fruits. Do men gather grapes . . ."
4. " But when thou doest alms " (that is, when you do any good thing) " let not your left hand know . . ."
5. " Inasmuch as ye have done it unto one of the least of these, my brethren . . ."
6. " Take no thought for the morrow . . . sufficient unto the day . . ."
7. " I came not to call the righteous . . ."
8. " For what is a man profited, if he shall gain the whole world . . ."
9. " Heaven and earth shall pass away but . . ."
10. " All things whatsoever ye would that men should do to you . . ."

THINGS JESUS SAID: RECORDED BY MARK

One of the things Mark tells us about Jesus' teaching is (Mark 12: 27) that " the common people heard him gladly." Can you continue the following quotations? Give the " sense ": it is not always necessary to give the exact wording.

1. " The Sabbath was made for man and . . ."
2. " If a house be divided against itself . . ."
3. " A prophet is not without honor but . . ."
4. " Whosoever will come after me, let him . . ."
5. " If any man desire to be first . . ."

72   [Answers on pages 75–76]

6. " Suffer the little children to come unto me and forbid them not, for . . ."

7. " For even the Son of man came not to be ministered unto but . . ."

8. " Ye have the poor with you always . . . but . . ."

9. " Watch and pray, lest ye enter into temptation. The spirit truly is ready . . ."

10. " Go ye into all the world . . ."

THINGS JESUS SAID: RECORDED BY LUKE

Continue, if you can, the quotations.

1. " Man shall not live by bread alone but . . ."

2. " Why beholdest thou the mote that is in thy brother's eye . . . but . . ."

3. " Why call ye me Lord, Lord, and . . ."

4. " Whosoever hath to him shall be given and whosoever hath not . . ."

5. " Whosoever will save his life shall lose it: but whosoever . . ."

6. " No man having put his hand to the plow and looking back . . ."

7. " The harvest truly is great . . ."

8. " Take heed and beware of covetousness; for a man's life . . ."

9. " Consider the lilies how they grow; they toil not neither do they spin; and yet I say unto you . . ."

10. In the gospel of Luke Jesus mentions by name at least a dozen Old Testament characters. Can you name four of them?

THINGS JESUS SAID: RECORDED BY JOHN

Continue, if you can, the quotations.

1. " God sent not his Son into the world to condemn the world . . ."

2. " God is a spirit and they that worship him . . ."

3. " My meat is to do . . ."

4. " He that is without sin among you . . ."

[Answers on pages 76–77]   **73**

5. " I must work the works of him that sent me, while it is day . . ."
6. " I am the resurrection and the life . . ."
7. " A new commandment I give unto you, that . . ."
8. " Greater love hath no man than this, that . . ."
9. " Ye are my friends if . . ."
10. " And this is life eternal . . ."

[Answers on page 77]

ANSWERS

THE BEST OF THE BIBLE

No. 1. THINGS THAT JESUS DID

1. Until he was thirty, he almost certainly worked as a carpenter for the support of the members of the family: his mother and his brothers and sisters.

2. Luke tells us of his reading aloud in the synagogue of his home town, Nazareth.

3. He took them in his arms and blessed them. Mark 10: 16.

4. Nowhere does the Bible say so. For this reason many people have said that he never *was* sick. More than one verse implies that at times he was very tired. Matt. 26: 37.

5. He did. Matt. 17: 24–27.

6. Our only record of Jesus' writing is of a time when he stooped down and wrote with his finger upon the ground. John 8: 6.

7. Often and sometimes sternly. Not only did he warn groups of people but personal friends as well—Peter for instance.

8. It would seem that he did. In Matthew's account of the Last Supper, we are told, "And when they had sung an hymn, they went out into the Mount of Olives." Matt. 26: 30.

9. This question may seem fantastic but, in reading John 21. it seems probable that he did.

10. He "went about doing good." Acts 10: 38.

No. 2. THINGS JESUS SAID: RECORDED BY MATTHEW

1. ". . . but lay up for yourselves treasures in heaven." Matt. 6: 19–20.

2. ". . . that ye be not judged." Matt. **7: 1.**

3. ". . . of thorns or figs of thistles." Matt. **7: 16.**

4. ". . . know what thy right hand doeth." Matt. **6: 3.**
Jesus was saying, " *Never* do a good thing to show off: to do that
spoils it—it isn't any longer a good thing."

5. ". . . ye have done it unto me." Matt. 25: 40.

6. ". . . is the evil thereof." Matt. 6: 34. In other words,
" Don't worry."

7. ". . . but sinners to repentance." Matt. 9: 13.

8. ". . . and lose his own soul." Matt. 16: 26.

9. ". . . my words shall not pass away." Matt. 24: 35.

10. ". . . do ye even so to them; for this is the law and the
prophets." Matt. 7: 12.

No. 3. THINGS JESUS SAID: RECORDED BY MARK

1. ". . . not man for the Sabbath." Mark 2: 27.

2. ". . . that house cannot stand." Mark 3: 25.

3. ". . . in his own country." Mark 6: 4.

4. ". . . deny himself, and take up his cross, and follow me."
Mark 8: 34.

5. ". . . he shall be the last of all and the servant of all."
Mark 9: 35.

6. ". . . of such is the kingdom of heaven." Mark 10: 14.

7. ". . . to minister, and to give his life a ransom for many."
Mark 10: 45.

8. ". . . me ye have not always." Mark 14: 7.

9. ". . . but the flesh is weak." Mark 14: 38.

10. ". . . and preach the gospel to every creature." Mark
J6: 15.

No. 4. THINGS JESUS SAID: RECORDED BY LUKE

1. ". . . by every word of God." Luke 4: 4.

2. ". . . but perceivest not the beam that is in thine own
eye." Luke 6: 41.

3. ". . . do not the things that I say? " Luke 6: 46.

4. ". . . from him shall be taken even that which he seem-
eth to have." Luke 8: 18.

5. ". . . will lose his life for my sake shall find it." Luke 9: 24.

6. ". . . is fit for the kingdom of God." Luke 9: 62.

7. ". . . but the laborers are few." Luke 10: 2.

8. ". . . consisteth not in the abundance of the things which he possesseth." Luke 12: 15.

9. ". . . that Solomon in all his glory was not arrayed like one of these." Luke 12: 27.

10. Old Testament characters whom Jesus names are: 1. Abraham. 2. Noah. 3. Lot. 4. Isaac. 5. Jacob. 6. Moses. 7. David. 8. Solomon. 9. Elijah. 10. Elisha. 11. Naaman. 12. Jonah.

No. 5. THINGS JESUS SAID: RECORDED BY JOHN

1. ". . . but that the world through him might be saved." John 3: 17.

2. ". . . must worship him in spirit and in truth." John 4: 24.

3. ". . . the will of him that sent me and finish his work." John 4: 34.

4. ". . . let him first cast a stone at her." John 8: 7.

5. ". . . the night cometh when no man can work." John 9: 4.

6. ". . . he that believeth on me, though he were dead, yet shall he live." John 11: 25.

7. ". . . that ye love one another." John 13: 34.

8. ". . . a man lay down his life for his friends." John 15: 13.

9. ". . . ye do whatsoever I command you." John 15: 14.

10. ". . . and that they might know thee, the only true God, and Jesus Christ, whom thou hast sent." John 17: 3.

THE "ENCYCLOPEDIA" QUIZZES

"Read not to contradict and confute," said a great British essayist, "not to believe and take for granted, nor to find talk and discourse, but to weigh and consider."

The Bible may be read in many ways.

A childish, though once common, way is to take it as a book of magic, of charms and incantations for working miracles. Thus some people have thought that the Bible would tell them exactly what to do if they opened it at random and read the first verse upon which their eyes fell. A better way, surely, would be to consider a puzzling question thoughtfully and prayerfully.

One may read the Bible as he would read any other book: there is no irreverence in reading the account of St. Paul's shipwreck as you would that of Robinson Crusoe—as a thrilling story of adventure; or in reading the 19th Psalm as you would read any other great poem. The Bible may be studied as one would study any other book. Or it may be read (and studied) as one would read and study *no* other book—as a lamp to the feet, a light to the path.

Also, one may use the Bible as he would an encyclopedia, searching it for information about this or that: a very important use too, because it is so easy to fool ourselves and, by taking only verses that please us, make the Bible say whatever we want it to. The quizzes that follow do not of course "settle" any of the questions raised. To do that would require far deeper study.

No. 1. WHAT DOES THE BIBLE TEACH ABOUT WAR AND PEACE?

Hundreds of books have been written seeking to give a final answer to this question. The questions that follow offer a beginning for study.

78   [Answers on page 82]

1. What is the attitude of most Old Testament writers to war?

2. In one of his greatest poems, Lord Alfred Tennyson foretold world peace (as well as the airplane): ". . . the Parliament of Man, the Federation of the world." Does the Bible anywhere prophesy world peace?

3. Did Jesus himself ever use violence?

4. What did Jesus say should be our feeling toward our enemies?

5. What did Jesus say about obedience to governmental authority?

6. Does Jesus anywhere prophesy that wars will continue?

7. Did Jesus ever advise his followers to arm themselves?

8. Who said, " All that take the sword shall perish by the sword," and under what circumstances?

No. 2. WHAT DOES THE BIBLE TEACH ABOUT " LABOR AND CAPITAL "?

A half dozen references, out of many that might be cited.

1. Is business success commended in the Bible?

2. As an example of hard, steady work, the Proverbs point us to what insect?

3. In the Old Testament many verses represent wealth as a blessing. What did Jesus say implying that it is very dangerous?

4. In the Old Testament, " usury " (which there means interest) is forbidden to the Jewish people. Did Jesus ever say anything that would seem to conflict with this?

5. Who said " the laborer is worthy of his hire " ?

6. One of the parables of Jesus, it has been contended, teaches that men should be paid according to their need, rather than according to the amount of work done. What is the parable?

No. 3. WHAT DOES THE BIBLE TEACH ABOUT TEMPTATION?

1. The Tempter is " subtile." He can tempt one in all sorts of seeming-pleasant ways: æsthetically—through one's love of

[Answers on pages 82–83]

the beautiful; intellectually—through his desire for knowledge; physically—through his appetites. He can tell much truth—mixed with just enough falsehood to make it poisonous. He can insinuate: "Punishment? Consequences? Never fear. It won't happen to you. You can 'get by.'" All this is illustrated in the story of the first temptation—that of the forbidden tree. How does it make all of the appeals mentioned above?

2. How would you define temptation?

3. May one say that God has tempted him?

4. Aside from his temptation in the wilderness, does the Bible tell us anything of Jesus' temptations?

5. May a temptation be so strong that one is not to blame, if he yields to it?

6. What is a good way of meeting temptations?

7. Should we be alarmed and troubled, if we find ourselves tempted?

8. When a friend is tempted and falls, how should we feel and act about it?

9. The Lord's Prayer contains what petition about temptation?

No. 4. WHAT DOES THE BIBLE TEACH ABOUT GIVING?

1. Almost incidentally, Jesus once said something implying (what the Old Testament clearly states—Deut. 15: 11) that there will always be need for private charity. What was it?

2. What elsewhere unrecorded saying of Jesus' did Paul quote about giving and receiving?

3. Did Jesus ever command giving?

4. Does the Bible anywhere tell us that it "pays" to be generous?

5. Writing to friends in Corinth, Paul gave what advice about systematic giving?

6. We are not to give "grudgingly or of necessity." Why?

No. 5. WHAT DOES THE BIBLE TEACH ABOUT SIN?

Sin is not a popular word in our day. (It probably never was.) The Bible however has a good deal to say about it.

[Answers on pages 83–84]

1. "The sin of doing nothing," some one has said, "is the worst of all the seven deadly sins." What verse in the Bible says much the same thing?

2. In Jesus' picture of the Last Judgment, the wicked are punished for just one thing. What?

3. Do you recall any Old Testament passage in which forgiveness of sins is promised?

4. The Bible tells us that the wages of sin is—what?

5. What did John the Baptist tell the sinners of his generation that they ought to do?

6. Did Jesus ever claim that he could forgive sins?

No. 6. WHAT DOES THE BIBLE TEACH ABOUT LIFE AFTER DEATH?

1. Some verses in the Old Testament seem to imply that there is no life after death. What story from early Jewish history would seem to contradict this belief?

2. In what is probably the most familiar of all Old Testament passages, death is referred to as something that need not be feared. What are the words?

3. Jesus once told his friends not to fear death but at once added a caution. What were his words?

4. What Bible writer tells us most about the resurrection of the dead?

5. Where in the Bible do we find the fullest description of Heaven?

6. If you had a friend who, knowing himself about to die, asked you to read aloud to him a passage from the Bible, what would you choose?

[Answers on pages 84–85]   **81**

ANSWERS

THE "ENCYCLOPEDIA" QUIZZES

No. 1. WHAT DOES THE BIBLE TEACH ABOUT WAR AND PEACE?

1. They seem to take it for granted. Verses could be cited condoning and sometimes commanding war—even wars of aggression.

2. Yes. In the sublime and beautiful second chapter of Isaiah, among other places: ". . . nation shall not lift up sword against nation, neither shall they learn war any more."

3. John 2: 14–15 tells of a scourge of small cords, with which he drove the money changers from the temple. What degree of violence this involved we are not told.

4. " But I say unto you, ' Love your enemies.' " Matt. 5: 44.

5. " Render therefore unto Caesar the things that are Caesar's and unto God the things that are God's." Mark 12: 17. (There remains of course the question: What things *are* God's and what Caesar's?)

6. He says (Matt. 24: 6) : " Ye shall hear wars and rumors of wars; " and immediately adds, " See that ye be not troubled."

7. Yes. Luke 22: 36. ". . . he that hath no sword let him sell his garment and buy one." Much has been written about these words which, it should be recalled, were spoken to a special group at a special time. Quite evidently they puzzled those to whom they were spoken.

8. Jesus spoke the words to Peter, when he drew his sword and wounded the servant of the high priest.

No. 2. WHAT DOES THE BIBLE TEACH ABOUT " LABOR AND CAPITAL " ?

1. Yes. Among other places in Prov. 22: 29. " Seest thou a

man diligent in his business? He shall stand before kings: he shall not stand before mean men."

2. "Go to the ant, thou sluggard, consider her ways and be wise." Prov. 6: 6.

3. "It is easier for a camel to pass through the eye of a needle than for a rich man to enter into the kingdom of God . . . but with God all things are possible." Matt. 19: 24–26.

4. The parables of the talents and the pounds (Matt. 25 and Luke 19) both tell of making a profit on investments and it is not condemned.

5. Jesus—in sending out the seventy. Luke 10: 7.

6. The parable of the laborers in the vineyard. Matt. 20.

No. 3. WHAT DOES THE BIBLE TEACH ABOUT TEMPTATION?

1. The tree was (1) "pleasant to the eyes;" (2) "a tree to be desired, to make one wise;" (3) "good for food." Gen. 3: 6.

2. Perhaps the best definition is: the call of one's lower as opposed to his higher nature. Jas. 1: 14.

3. James says no. "Let no man say, when he is tempted, 'I am tempted of God.'" Jas. 1: 13.

4. The writer of the Epistle to the Hebrews says that he "was tempted in all points like as we are, yet without sin."

5. Paul says (I Cor. 10: 13): "But God is faithful, who will not suffer you to be tempted above that ye are able but will with the temptation make a way of escape."

6. Jesus (Matt. 4) remembered his early teaching, the things he had learned in the Bible.

7. James says: "Count it all joy, when ye fall into divers temptations." (Jas. 1: 2.) One's feeling, he seems to say, should be that of a soldier rejoicing in a particularly dangerous assignment.

8. Paul says (Gal. 6: 1): ". . . restore such an one in the spirit of meekness; considering thyself, lest thou also be tempted."

9. "Lead us not into temptation."

No. 4. WHAT DOES THE BIBLE TEACH ABOUT GIVING?

1. "Ye have the poor always with you." Matt. 26: 11.

2. "Remember the words of the Lord Jesus, how he said, 'It is more blessed to give than to receive.'" Acts 20: 35.

3. Yes, in the Sermon on the Mount: "Give to him that asketh and from him that would borrow of thee turn not thou away." Matt. 5: 42.

4. Yes, in a number of places in both the Old and New Testaments. "Give and it shall be given unto you; good measure, pressed down, shaken together and running over . . ." Luke 6: 38. "He that hath pity on the poor lendeth to the Lord: and that which he hath given will he repay him again." Prov. 19: 17.

5. "Upon the first day of the week, let every one of you lay by him in store, as God hath prospered him." I Cor. 16: 2.

6. "For God loveth a cheerful giver." II Cor. 9: 7.

No. 5. WHAT DOES THE BIBLE TEACH ABOUT SIN?

1. To him that knoweth to do good and doeth it not, to him it is sin." Jas. 4: 17. There are of course other perfectly correct definitions: for example, "Sin is the transgression of the law." I John 3: 4.

2. For their failure to do the kind and helpful things they might have done. Matt. 25: 31–46.

3. The most famous and beautiful is probably that from Isaiah 1: "Though your sins be as scarlet, they shall be white as snow; though they be red like crimson, they shall be as wool."

4. ". . . the wages of sin is death." Rom. 6: 23.

5. "Repent, for the kingdom of heaven is at hand." To a group whom he considered especially sinful, he added: "Bring forth fruits meet for repentance." Matt. 3: 2–8.

6. He did. "But that ye may know that the Son of man hath power on earth to forgive sin . . ." Mark 2: 10.

No. 6. WHAT DOES THE BIBLE TEACH ABOUT LIFE AFTER DEATH?

1. The raising of Samuel by the Witch of Endor. I Sam. 28.

2. " Yea, though I walk through the valley of the shadow of death, I will fear no evil." Psalm 23.

3. " Fear not them which kill the body . . . but rather fear him which is able to destroy both soul and body in hell." Matt. 10: 28.

4. Paul. See in particular I Cor. 15.

5. In the last chapters of the book of Revelation.

6. There is of course no one correct answer to this question. A man who has more than once performed this service told me he had read Isaiah 35. My own choice would be the fourteenth chapter of John: " Let not your heart be troubled," etc.

RETOLD BIBLE STORIES

No. 1. THE WATCHER

I was a mere slip of a girl then and yet, in the space of less than an hour, I did the most useful thing I ever did—something worth more than all the rest of all the work of all my life. I who have lived long and had a part in many great events.

It was during the period of our most cruel oppression and a child in such times learns with unbelievable quickness to conceal and dissimulate. Thus I had known from the beginning that my wee brother had no right to be born, though the harsh law against our race was to be sure not strictly enforced. (Men are seldom quite as bad as their worst laws.) But we took no chances and week after week, excepting a few of our own people, no one knew that our house sheltered a baby.

The time came of course when we could no longer hide him and then mother contrived the thing she did, hoping perhaps that the unbelievable thing that did happen would happen. Out of materials nearest to hand, she fashioned a sort of floating cradle and laid the baby in it. At a carefully selected spot, we placed it among the rushes in the slack water of the river, where it would not float away. Then, with what thoughts you may imagine, she turned and went slowly home—leaving me on guard. I was to see that no harm came to our little ship and its precious cargo.

At the first sight of the great ladies in their splendid array, I was frightened. Yet I could not believe *they* would harm a baby and I waited with beating heart, making myself small as I could crouching there among the rushes.

They saw our " ark " (they could hardly fail to see it) and she who seemed their mistress sent one of them to bring it. Crowding about it, they turned back the cover and then for a moment I was worried, for he cried and no one wants a baby to do that. I crept nearer but all watching him (he was a pretty baby) they did not see me and so it was that I heard kind words and knew that no harm was going to come to him, that she who was first among them meant to keep him and care for him.

All at once I was very bold and very sly. I went straight to her and looked up into her face. She was a great lady, I reminded her, she could not of course care for the baby herself. Should I go and find a nurse for her? Then, when she said yes, I went and brought mother.

She who adopted him and called him her son was a princess and whether she ever guessed that his "nurse" was his real mother I do not know. She had him trained in all the wisdom of her people: such an education as never came to any other of our despised race. That was part of his rearing for the high destiny God had in store for him.

By what a slender thread the fate of a nation hung that afternoon! An "ark" of bullrushes and, upon the river bank, a little girl watching.

1. Who tells the story?
2. What was her brother's name?
3. The name of the river?
4. What "princess" adopted him?
5. What was his "high destiny"?
6. Whereabouts in the Bible is the story found?

No. 2. THE HOME-COMING

It was in the beginning of the barley harvest that we came, the two of us, to the little home town that I had left so many years before. It was not greatly changed—the town itself: but among the people—who was not changed? Some whom I recalled as little girls playing about the streets were now carrying in their arms babies of their own. Boys mischievous and active, the age of my own when we went away, were now grown to bronzed, bearded men, doing their full share of heavy work among the harvesters. Those who had once been most active in all village doings were now grown old: and the old—how many of them were missing!

Yet not a few remained who remembered and welcomed me, calling me by the pleasant, undeserved name that had been given me in babyhood. They remembered the circumstances of our leaving (a sad time for them too) and wished to know how the Lord had dealt with me in the land whither I had gone. Alas, it was a sad story I must tell them: years of exile—sons and husband no longer mine—only three graves far away among the purple hills beyond the river. Now I was come back—an old woman.

Yet, in the faces of old friends and in their sympathy, my heart found comfort. All were kind to me. All wished to be helpful. But I asked nothing of any one, even of my dead husband's rich kinsman. The years had taught me to fend for myself and count little upon others. Besides, the well-to-do have so many calls upon them. Why should he trouble himself about a poor widow, whom in all likelihood he had wholly forgotten?

My first thought, naturally, was for her who had left everything to come with me. These days were a knitting up of old ties for me but for her everything was new and unfamiliar. Brave and resolute as she was, she must feel herself a stranger in a strange land. Only too well did I know that feeling and I dreaded for her the homesickness that I felt must surely come some time. My own struggles to adapt myself to new surroundings had not always been easy. Nor did I ever forget that love of me and nothing else had made her take the long journey and never once speak of turning back. I could not bear that she should some day regret it, she who was still young, for whom life ought to hold something more. So as best I could I sought to plan for her. Sometimes I was grateful, I confess, because we had so little: to win our daily bread kept us busy—there was no time for brooding.

Anxious, troubled days. How little could I foresee what God had planned for us. That near almost as sunrise there waited rich, happy days—some of the richest and happiest of our lives.

1. Who tells the story?
2. In what land had she been living?
3. Name the town to which she returned.
4. Who accompanied her?
5. Who was her husband's well-to-do kinsman?
6. To what period of Jewish history does the story belong?

 [Answers on page 103]

No. 3. NIGHT PATROL

Such a thing may happen once in a campaign—or a lifetime. To me it seemed a God-given chance and, had I had my way, the whole history of our people might have been different. But the young captain said no and, as a good soldier should, I obeyed orders. Still——! One spear thrust——! And, as I told him, the deed would not have been his. It would have been mine. Oh, well! He was a good soldier, yet always something of a dreamer—a poet. His harp playing showed that.

It happened in those days of disorder, when our little band was seeking safety anywhere it could find it and our scouts must be constantly on the alert. Dubious neighbors were always betraying us and, every time they reported us to the king, he like the mad man he was would once more set out in pursuit of us. A life of daily hardship and peril, yet we often enjoyed it, as children enjoy their games of hide and seek.

That night we knew exactly where the king's troop lay and the young captain, as eager for adventure as any of us, declared that he himself was going scouting. When he asked for some one to go with him, I naturally volunteered. I always enjoyed such patrolling. I knew too that he was apt to be venturesome and I wanted to spare him any unnecessary risk.

We crossed the considerable space that lay between our lines and theirs. When we reached the outskirts of their encampment, no one challenged us. Swiftly but cautiously we went on—wondering. Presently we stood, we two, looking down in the moonlight upon the sleeping king. Beside him, stuck into the ground, was his spear and a jug of water, in case he should waken in the night and wish to quench his thrist. His chief captain lay near him and round about, fast asleep, were a dozen of the bodyguard. Not a single sentry awake and on duty!

Then I whispered my suggestion. What a chance to end everything in our favor. Had not God himself led us to this moment? One spear thrust—I would not need to strike a second time—and the young captain would be free forever from his mortal enemy. Considering his popularity with the people, a throne lay that night within his grasp. Instead of taking it, he talked—while I listened impatiently—about the wickedness of destroying the Lord's anointed. As if, in his place, the king would have hesitated one moment!

Taking the spear and the water jug, we returned to our own lines. In the dawn, the young captain called across to them, holding up our trophies and deriding them for the lax guard they had kept. He asked what evil he had done and the king was for the moment melted—as he had been before. He was wrong, he said, he called him " my son." A perfect reconciliation, one might have thought. But I knew better and so, in his heart, did the young captain. He knew return to the court meant the risk of assassination. A few days respite and again we were in flight, with the king in pursuit of us.

1. Who tells the story?
2. Who was the " young captain " ?
3. Who was the king?
4. Who was his chief captain?
5. Whereabouts in the Bible is the story found?

No. 4.   A REAL ESTATE TRANSFER

I made the man a fair, even a generous, offer. I told him moreover, if mine seemed to him too little, to name his own price. It had no great intrinsic value, that miserable piece of earth the sight of which now fills me with loathing. Only, it was so near us and fitted so well into our plans for the enlargement of the palace grounds. The man should have sold. It would have saved so much trouble for every one.

Instead, like the stubborn boor he was, he only prated about the Lord forbidding that he part with the inheritance of his fathers. He might have made himself a rich man, my heart was so set upon the purchase. He might have stopped to consider that I was his king—that I could have dealt with him sternly. He was not to be moved—he would do nothing. Returning to the palace, bitterly disappointed, I lay down and refused to eat.

The queen, my wife, came to seek me and wanted to know why I was troubled. She, I might tell you, had been reared in other surroundings than mine, where kingship was less hampered by

90

[Answers on page 103]

old customs and tribal traditions. When I told her of my refused offer, she laughed at me. Indeed I knew she despised me for so tamely accepting defeat at the hands of a subject. She bid me eat and be merry. The whole thing was absurdly simple: leave it all to her. There would, she assured me, be no trouble at all about it. So I tried to dismiss it from my mind, though suspecting, I confess, that she would use harsher measures than I would.

Not long after she came to me, saying the property now was mine. All I need do was go down and possess it. What she had done —— I will not say I was ignorant of it but I did not inquire too closely.

I was there in the vineyard, planning the new uses for it, when I saw him—the one man I have ever most dreaded.

" Hast thou found me, O mine enemy? " I asked him.

He flung at me such words that one would have thought he was the king and I a cowering criminal. He foretold things I tremble to remember and swore that they would be meted out to me by the God of our fathers, whose law of righteousness I had scorned. I felt myself weak as water, powerless to raise a hand against him, or even to order his arrest.

Now, again, I eat nothing. I feel the sackcloth upon my flesh and sit with rent garments and ashes upon my head. Perhaps, if not averted, they may be delayed a while—these evils he has foretold against me.

1. Who tells the story?
2. Who was his queen?
3. Who was the man defrauded?
4. Who accused the king of his crime?
5. Whereabouts in the Bible is the story found?

No. 5. THE PROPHET'S SERVANT

I stood high in the favor of my master: it was even thought that one day I would be his successor. He shared with me his confidence and more than once sent me on important missions. I reverenced him and I never questioned his greatness. Certainly I do not now doubt it. Only, he seemed to me often quite impractical. In some ways, I felt myself far wiser than he. Why

[Answers on pages 103–104]   91

not use to his own profit his great gifts? Not that I would have had him perform miracles for hire but —— When one begged him to take a gift—as a favor ——!

Then this happened:

I was there when, sent on by the king at my master's bidding, the great general from the country of our ally came bringing with him the royal letter. I saw his horses and chariots at our door and heard the message which my master sent out to him. I could understand something of his resentment. My master could not have given a better example of his other-worldliness. A distinguished foreigner! A personal greeting—that much of deference was surely due him.

I followed when at the urging of his servants he finally humbled himself and went down to our despised river. I saw his incredulous wonder when he recognized the completeness of the cure he had so nearly refused to try. I was there when he returned to my master—he and all his retinue. Then indeed my master saw him and they talked together—about the worship of Jehovah. The great man begged him to accept what he called a "blessing" and my master (characteristically) refused it.

When they were gone, I followed after. Why, a king's ransom had been thrust upon us, enough to make a man rich for all his days: and my master had turned aside, as if it were nothing. The great man saw me coming, recognized me and himself stepped down from his chariot to receive me. I told my plausible story. He never questioned it but cheerfully gave me more than I had asked for. He bid two of his servants carry it for me. At a convenient place, I dismissed them, hid my treasure and went in again before my master.

Where had I been? he asked me. I was frightened then but what was there to do, save to deny that I had been anywhere? Then he told me everything that had happened—told it as if he had seen it with his own eyes. (Perhaps he had!) Sternly he pronounced upon me my sentence of punishment. And now ——! I have all the great general gave me. Money! Rich clothing! Of what use are they to one afflicted as I am?

1. Who tells the story?
2. Who was his master?

92　　　　　　　　　　　　　　　　　　　[Answers on page 104]

3. Who was " the great general " ?
4. Of what disease was he healed?
5. Whereabouts in the Bible is the story found?

No. 6. THE MAN WHO SUFFERED

I was a rich man, living outside the borders of Palestine. I had vast herds of cattle—sheep, oxen, camels. It was said of me that I was the greatest of all the men of the east. Fortunate also was I in my home life, with sons and daughters who had grown up to be an increasing joy to their father. My reputation was that of a man who was upright, feared God and eschewed evil.

Many must have envied me, until a certain day when from every quarter of the heaven calamity fell upon me: fire—tempest—bereavement—the invasion of enemies! That one day stripped me of everything: family, vast possessions and reputation. Sickness followed—a disease so loathsome that death would have brought welcome release.

In time of trouble one looks to his friends. Three of mine came to visit me. I had hope that they might bring consolation and they did at first—a little. Seeing how great was my grief, they sat a long while and said nothing. At last I spoke and, when they sought to answer me, they proved miserable comforters—all of them. For them my sufferings had only one possible meaning. My life, they acknowledged, had seemed to be upright but this impression must certainly have been deceptive. I must, in secret, have committed some great sin. Now all this was come upon me as a punishment. How could it be otherwise? Did God send such evils without a reason? Surely not. If only I would seek peace through repentance and confession! Such counsel I resented for, searching my heart, I found no great sin—certainly nothing to match my sufferings. Long and bitterly we argued the matter.

Then, while we spoke, there came to us a voice out of the whirlwind and it was the voice of God.

Prosperity, after many days, returned to me. Again I was rich, happy, honored and out of my suffering I had learned something. No man is wise enough to make clear to his fellows all

[Answers on page 104]   93

God's purposes. Who can "understand" him, whose ways are not our ways, are indeed "past finding out." But one *may* know him (better sometimes through suffering than through joy) and, knowing him, may come to love and trust him, as a little child loves and trusts its parents.

1. Who tells the story?
2. Where did he live?
3. Can you name at least one of his three friends?
4. What is the literary form in which his story is told in the Bible?
5. What is its central theme?

No. 7. THE FISHERMAN

Through the long hours of the night, the four of us, my brother, our two partners and I, had been fishing and we were dead tired. Even more tired in spirit, I think, than in body for we had had no luck—had taken absolutely nothing. It is like that sometimes in our business: one would say that the fish had formed a league against us. Now the nets must be washed and we were busy with them when the crowd came—such a crowd as was always following the Young Prophet.

As he talked to them, we ourselves stopped to listen and, listening, forgot something of our weariness. The crowd grew ever larger and pressed upon him until I was fearful that some one would be pushed into the water. He too must have noticed it for presently he stopped to ask me if he might have the loan of an empty boat. I was of course glad to let him have mine. He was a man for whom it was a joy to do favors and, at his request, I thrust out a little way from land and there cast anchor. In that way practically every one could see and hear him and there was little danger of an accident. He sat in the stern, talking to them and they listened eagerly, as the common people always listened to him.

After he had finished speaking and had dismissed them, he turned to us and suggested that I go out for another draught. I told him of our long night of fruitless toil and that another trial seemed to me perfectly useless. (He himself was not a fisher-

94   [Answers on page 104]

man but had followed the trade of a carpenter.) He seemed serenely confident, as if he foresaw what would happen but I went chiefly, as I recall, because I wished to be courteous to him.

At our first cast, we enclosed such a school of fish that the net broke and my brother and I had to summon our partners in the other boat. Even so, we had like to have been swamped in landing them. I was frightened, for never in all my years of fishing had I seen anything like it. I told him to leave me—I was not fit to associate with a man like him. Instead he talked with us and ended by asking us—all four of us—to come with him and help him in his great work. He would, he said, make us " catch men." It was long before we understood all he meant by that but we followed him, proudly and gladly.

1. Who tells the story?
2. Who was the brother mentioned?
3. Who were the partners?
4. Where had they been fishing?
5. Whereabouts in the Bible is the story found?

No. 8. THE SORCERER

Men not only enjoy being deceived, they will pay liberally him who deceives them. I should know, I live by my wits and I could give you a hundred examples from my own experience. At times this whole city has rung with my praise and I have deserved it—I know I am good in my field. But that very fact made me quick to recognize one who was better.

He came from the south, preaching the new doctrine of those who later came to be known as Christians. What he said interested me little but the things he did were startling and all could see them. I knew of course there was some trick to it and set myself to learn his secret. When it proved not as easy as I had hoped, I professed myself one of his followers. Being freely accepted, I spent much time with him, trying to find out not only how he performed his wonders but what there was in it for him. I was able to learn nothing. The man's methods baffled me completely and he was as likely to heal a beggar as a millionaire. None the less, I remained patient, watchful and undiscouraged.

[Answers on page 104]   95

They later told us that two of the leaders of the new sect would come up from Jerusalem and that stirred in me a new interest. Now, at last I might get somewhere. This first man, astonishing as he was, might well be only a neophyte, an underling.

When they came, I met them, watched them but again could discover nothing—I who would have said I knew every device of my difficult profession. I gave up at last and went to him who was their leader, owning my defeat. There was of course some trick, I told him (there always is), and, if he would teach me, I was sure I could learn it. He was a poor man (that any one could see) and I was able to pay liberally.

I found quickly there was no doing business with him. He turned upon me with such blistering words as I had never imagined could come from his lips. He called me a bitter poison, a bundle of iniquity and bid me take my money with me to destruction. I, who have faced a hundred critical situations, found myself at last cowering at his feet, begging that he would entreat the powers he served to spare me the dreadful things he threatened. He made no promises. An outcast from their brotherhood, I still wake at night sometimes, hearing his voice and trembling, dreading the unknown.

Are there men to whom money means nothing? Men who will toil like slaves, go hungry, endure stripes and imprisonment (as some of these men have) and ask for it nothing that any man can see or feel? Men who rejoice to suffer for some cause that to them is holy? Who live, move, have their being in an unseen world to which I am deaf and blind?

1. Who tells the story?
2. From his name is derived a common noun in criminology. What is it?
3. Who was the first preacher of the Christian faith to whom he attached himself?
4. Who were the two who came from Jerusalem?
5. Whereabouts in the Bible is the story found?

No. 9. THE LEGIONARY

For how many years we had been quartered among the Jewish people I do not now recall but it was long enough for my

 [Answers on page 104]

master to become impressed with their form of worship and finally to be converted to it. In that I followed him, partly because of his example, partly because the new religion appealed to me as more reasonable than that in which I had been reared.

My master was as fine a man and a soldier as any I ever knew and I had served under him for many years. Now this new, shared religion formed another bond between us. We talked of it often and it was, I suppose, partly on account of it that I was detailed to special service in his home.

While we were stationed in Caesarea, he came to me one day, asking that I go for him on a special mission. I was to take two of the servants, go to a certain city not too far distant and there ask for a man whom my master had never seen but of whom he had been told in a vision. A divine command, he felt, had been laid upon him and, if possible, I was to bring this man back with me.

My master seemed to think he would surely come but, for my part, I had some misgivings. This man was a Jew and I had lived long enough among his people to know something of their strict regulations. A Jew may be friendly enough toward a " gentile " (that is what they call us), he may even gladly accept him as a " proselyte " but to come to his house—to eat with him—that may be strictly forbidden by his religion. But of all this I said nothing to my master.

We started next morning, made our journey without adventure and found the man just where my master had been told in his vision that we would find him—in the home of a friend living by the seaside. I delivered my message, taking good care to tell him how good a man my master was and the high regard in which he was held by the Jews of Caesarea.

We were courteously received (so much I had expected) and they provided us with lodging for the night. On the morrow we set forth and, to my surprise, the man made no objection to coming with us. Arrived in Caesarea, where my master had gathered a number of friends and relatives to receive him, he confessed that his coming had been contrary to the rules of his faith but he had, he said, come to question the rightness of those rules.

Religion, he now knew, was a growing thing. For three years

he had been the close companion of the greatest of all religious teachers, yet he had not mastered his teachings perfectly. A new lesson had been taught him on the day that we came knocking at his door.

1. Who was " my master " ?
2. To whom was the narrator sent?
3. In what city did he find him?
4. What " new lesson " had just been taught him?
5. Whereabouts in the Bible is the story found?

No. 10. A JAIL DELIVERY

Going from place to place, telling the good news and seeing the lives of men transformed by it—who could ask for anything better? Especially fortunate was I too in my travelling companion, a man who had planted the good seed in many widely scattered fields and remained on fire with eagerness to carry it farther. I was proud to be associated with him and in this new city the beginning of our work had been auspicious.

Our people had no synagogue there but on the Sabbath we went outside the gates to a place of prayer upon the river bank. There we found some devout women gathered and talked with them. One who became a follower of our Master persuaded us to stay at her home. We made new friends daily and no one sought to hinder us.

Then came the disturbing incident of the slave girl. She had annoyed us by following us and calling after us and one day my friend turned and sharply rebuked the spirit within her. Her masters, it seemed, had made her ravings a source of income. When this was cut off, they sought explanations and these led to us.

We were seized and dragged before the magistrates. Foreigners that we were, the girl's owners declared, we were disturbing the peace of the city and teaching practices unlawful for Romans. An absurd charge and utterly false of course but there was no reasoning with the mob and we were stripped, beaten and thrown into prison.

In one of his many letters, my friend speaks of " glorying " in tribulation. We did so that night. We were in pain, our feet

98   [Answers on pages 104–105]

fast in the stocks. We were prisoners, awaiting an uncertain morrow. Yet our hearts swelled with such rejoicing that we could not have kept from singing our hymns of triumphant praise. Our fellow prisoners listened and, I think, enjoyed it.

When the earthquake came, my friend was the most self-possessed man in the prison and his call to the jailor stopped the panic-stricken man from committing suicide. A wonderful night! From prisoners, we were suddenly transformed to honored guests. The man listened eagerly to all we had to tell him and accepted it joyfully.

When with morning word came that we might go free, my companion showed that stern trait which often stood him in good stead. Did the magistrates, he demanded, ask us to slink away secretly? We, who were Romans, had been beaten without trial and publicly. If they had now decided that we were innocent, let them at least give us a public acquittal and vindication. Frightened, they hastened to comply.

It seemed best we should go on to other fields but behind us we left good seed, growing richly in the hearts of good friends. Our stay in that city never seemed to us a defeat: it was a victory.

1. Who tells the story?
2. Who was his travelling companion?
3. In what city did the incident take place?
4. Who was the woman who entertained them in her home?
5. Whereabouts in the Bible is the story found?

No. 11. THE NEAR-RIOT

The thing has brought me plenty of unwelcome publicity and I have had a lot of explaining to do but, right here and now, I want to say that I was always one hundred percent for our city and our goddess and, really, I was not to blame for all that happened.

Like any business man, I did not like to have my business interfered with. These men whom I accused—well, I did not to be sure know a great deal about them but the little I did know was bad. They said—just imagine! Or at least I *heard* they said that gods made by human hands were no gods at all. Well,

[Answers on page 105]   99

making such gods, or rather making their shrines, is my trade, I employ a lot of workmen. My competitors do too and people from all the world come and buy the shrines and carry them home as charms and souvenirs. I did not want to see good men thrown out of work and a whole business ruined by a lot of crazy trouble-makers.

So (and this I have never denied) I called together some of the men of my own craft and told them what I thought: that, if talk like this was allowed to go on unchecked, the time might come when not only would we have no business but even the temple of our great goddess—one of the seven wonders of the world— would be neglected and our city itself might no longer be the commercial center it now is. I put it straight to them and they saw it exactly as I saw it. They said they would start something. They did.

In less time than you would think it possible, the whole city was in an uproar. A mob gathered and laid hold of two men. (That, I assure you, was none of my doing.) They milled around, most of them having no idea what it was all about. Finally all rushed into the theatre (our largest public building) and there for two solid hours they did nothing but roar out their slogan.

A man tried to talk but they shouted him down. My fellow craftsmen and I had lost all the little control over them we ever had and I don't mind saying that I was worried.

At last the town recorder came and, when he managed to get a hearing, scolded us as if we had been misbehaving school boys. What did we mean, he asked, spending these hours bellowing things known to everybody and denied by no one. These men who had been handled so roughly (and that I learned later was true) were guilty of neither treason nor sacrilege. If I —— Yes, he mentioned me by name. If I or any of my friends had anything against anybody, the courts were set up on purpose to handle such cases and we should have applied to them. A turmoil like this was a disgrace. It might even come to the ears of the Emperor.

The whole unpleasant business has taught me one thing: it is a lot easier to raise a mob than to control it.

1. Who tells the story?

100

[Answers on page 105]

2. What was his business?
3. In what city did the near-riot occur?
4. What was the mob's slogan?
5. Who were " the crazy trouble-makers "?
6. Whereabouts in the Bible is the story found?

No. 12. MOB SCENE

Sudden, riotous flare-ups like that were common enough. (I never knew a people who could fight so much over their religion.) Word was brought me that the whole city was in an uproar and I lost no time in myself getting down into the mêlée.

A mob had dragged a man from the temple enclosure and seemed bent upon beating him to death. Getting him out of their hands was not difficult (a mob has no chance against disciplined troops) but, when I tried to find out the occasion of all the trouble, they poured out such a flood of violent contradictions that I could make nothing of it and in despair ordered him brought to our barracks. The press by this time was such that the soldiers had actually to carry him up the steps, the crowd at our heels barking, " Kill him! Kill him! "

At the top of the steps, he asked to speak to me and I was surprised for not only was his accent that of an educated man but his language was my own mother tongue. I told him I had supposed he was the leader of a band of cutthroats who of late had given us much trouble but he assured me he was a Jew, named the city of his birth and asked if he might address the people. I readily consented, curious I confess to see how he would handle a raging mob like that.

Surprisingly, he secured their full attention, partly perhaps because he was now speaking *their* mother tongue. He told them of his life and appeared to be defending himself against the charge of some sort of sacrilege too complicated for my foreign comprehension. They gave him an excellent hearing, until he let slip the word " gentile." Then once more bedlam broke loose and I signalled the soldiers to bring him in.

Following the usual routine, I gave orders to have him flogged and he was being strapped up when one of the captains came and whispered to me. I went to him at once.

[Answers on page 105]

" Are you a Roman? " I asked him.

He said he was and further questioning showed him to be free born. (My own citizenship cost me a pretty penny.) After that, there was of course no thought of flogging.

Next day he was examined before one of their religious courts and, I was told, met their questioning cleverly. Even so, they were soon in such a tumult that I sent a squad of soldiers down to rescue him.

A plot, I learned later, had been laid to assassinate him. (Why their deadly hatred of the man I never found out.) I therefore sent him with a suitable escort to Caesarea. What his religion was I have no idea but he certainly had courage, and ability, and good sense. Along with him I sent a letter to the governor that I am sure did him no harm.

1. Who tells the story?
2. What official position did he hold?
3. In what city was he stationed?
4. Whom did he rescue from the mob?
5. Whereabouts in the Bible is the story found?

ANSWERS

Section V

RETOLD BIBLE STORIES

No. 1. THE WATCHER

1. Miriam.
2. Moses.
3. The Nile.
4. The Bible describes her simply as "the daughter of Pharaoh."
5. The deliverance of his people from slavery.
6. In Exodus 2.

No. 2. THE HOME-COMING

1. Naomi.
2. Moab.
3. Bethlehem.
4. Ruth.
5. Boaz.
6. The time of the Judges. (See Ruth 1.)

No. 3. NIGHT PATROL

1. Abishai.
2. David.
3. Saul.
4. Abner.
5. I Samuel 26.

No. 4. A REAL ESTATE TRANSFER

1. King Ahab.
2. Jezebel.
3. Naboth.

4. Elijah.
5. I Kings 21.

No. 5. THE PROPHET'S SERVANT

1. Gehazi.
2. The Prophet Elisha.
3. Naaman the Syrian.
4. Leprosy.
5. II Kings 5.

No. 6. THE MAN WHO SUFFERED

1. Job.
2. The Land of Uz.
3. They were: Eliphaz, the Temanite; Bildad, the Shuhite; and Zophar, the Naamathite. See Job 2: 11. (Elihu, while not one of the three " friends," is one of the speakers.)
4. In the form of a drama, with prologue and epilogue—one of the greatest dramas of all literature.
5. The problem of evil—of undeserved suffering.

No. 7. THE FISHERMAN

1. The Apostle Peter.
2. Andrew. (See John 1: 40.)
3. James and John.
4. In the Sea of Galilee—here called Gennesaret.
5. In the Gospel of Luke—chapter 5.

No. 8. THE SORCERER

1. Simon Magus.
2. Simony: the crime of obtaining a sacred office by purchase.
3. Philip.
4. Peter and John.
5. In the Acts of the Apostles—chapter 8.

No. 9. THE LEGIONARY

1. Cornelius, " a centurion of the Italian band."

2. Peter.
3. Joppa.
4. That "God is no respecter of persons."
5. In the Acts of the Apostles—chapter 10.

No. 10. A JAIL DELIVERY

1. Silas.
2. Paul.
3. Philippi.
4. Lydia.
5. In the Acts of the Apostles—chapter 16.

No. 11. THE NEAR-RIOT

1. Demetrius.
2. He was a silversmith.
3. Ephesus.
4. "Great is Diana of the Ephesians!"
5. Paul and his fellow missionaries.
6. In the Acts of the Apostles—chapter 19.

No. 12. MOB SCENE

1. Claudius Lysias.
2. The Authorized Version calls him " the chief captain of the band; " in Goodspeed's translation he is called " the colonel of the regiment."
3. Jerusalem.
4. Paul.
5. In the Acts of the Apostles—chapters 21, 22 and 23.

THE BIBLE AND THE POETS

"The Bible," says an eminent and reverent American scholar, "is literature not dogma."

One may not agree with him: that depends partly upon what is meant by "dogma" but one thing is certain—the Bible *is* literature. Profoundly has it influenced the literatures of many lands and languages and one cannot know English literature who does not know the Bible. This is as true of our generation as of any other. To take an extreme instance: it would not, I believe, be difficult to cite passages from P. G. Wodehouse, Alexander Woollcott or Ogden Nash which can be understood only by reference to the Bible.

The following quotations are but a few of hundreds that might be given. Many of the questions are easy; others, admittedly hard, serve to show that the standard poets knew the Bible well.

Should you wish to keep score upon the following 75 questions, each correct answer may count 5. A perfect score would thus be 375: a score of 300 would be excellent.

No. 1.   THE BIBLE AND CHAUCER

1.   As one would expect, the "father of English poetry" cites the Bible many times. Can you explain the following citations?

> Rede eek of Joseph, and ther schal ye see
> Whethir dremes ben som tyme (I say nought alle)
> Warnyng of thinges that shul after falle.

Joseph interpreted "dremes" twice. To whom?

2.   Unto his lemman Delida he tolde
>   That in his heres all his strengthe lay;
>   And falsely to his foomen sche him solde . . .

Of whom is the poet speaking?

106   [Answers on page 117]

3.   Lo Abygaille, by good conseil how sche
        Savyd hir housbond Nabal, whan that he
        Schold han ben slayn.

Why was Nabal in danger of being " slayn " ?

4.   But sodeynly he left his dignite,
        I-lak a best him seemed for to be,
        And eet hay as an oxe, and lay
        In rayn. . . .

The humiliation of what great king is being described?

5.   . . . whan of Christ our king
        Was asked, what is troth or sothfastnesse,
        He not a worde answerde.

Who asked this question of Christ?

No. 2. THE BIBLE AND SHAKESPEARE

On my shelves is a book of several hundred pages, bearing the title " The Bible and Shakespeare." It shows (if any proof were needed) that the writings of Shakespeare would have been very different, had he not known his Bible.

1.   What says this fool of Hagar's offspring?

Shylock is speaking. Why should he think badly of Hagar's off-spring?

2.   I'll yield him thee asleep
        Where thou may'st knock a nail into his head.

Caliban (the speaker) knew of course nothing about the Bible but his offer instantly suggests a Bible story about—whom?

3. Samson, Master . . . he carried the town, gates on his
      back, like a porter.

What town gates?

4.   He falls like Lucifer, never to hope again.

What does the Bible say about Lucifer?

5. Whiles the mad mothers, with their howls confused,
      Do break the clouds, as did the wives of Jewry
      At Herod's blood-hunting slaughter men.

[Answers on page 117]

What event is referred to?

6. The Devil can cite Scripture for his purpose.
Did the Devil ever do so?

7. Shall I keep your hogs and eat husks with them?
What parable of Jesus' is suggested?

8. To smell pork, to eat of the habitation which your prophet, the Nazarite, conjured the devil into.
To what incident does Shylock refer?

9. Would any of the stock of Barabbas
   Had been her husband rather than a Christian.
Who was Barabbas?

10. A kissing traitor; How art thou prov'd Judas.
Why *kissing* traitor?

No. 3. THE BIBLE AND MILTON

One need hardly be reminded of the great poems of John Milton founded on Scriptural themes: *Paradise Lost, Paradise Regained* and *Samson Agonistes*—to cite no others.

1. What passion cannot Music raise and quell?
   When Jubal struck the chorded shell
   His listening brethren stood around
   And, wondering, on their faces fell
   To worship the celestial sound.

Why should Jubal be the one to strike the " chorded shell " ?

2. Peor and Baalim
   Forsake their temples dim,
   With the twice-batter'd god of Palestine . . .

Who was the " twice-battered " god?   (This is one of the harder questions.)

3. See how from far, upon the eastern road,
   The star-led wizards haste with odors sweet . . .

Who were the " star-led wizards " ?

  [Answers on pages 117–118]

4.   Full forty days he pass'd . . .
Nor tasted human food, nor hunger felt
Till those days ended, hunger'd then at last . . .

What is here described?

5.   Last came, and last to go,
The pilot of the Galilean Lake;
Two massy keys he bore . . .

Who was the pilot?

No. 4.   THE BIBLE AND COWPER

Cowper's Scriptural citations are to be found not only in his
hymns, some of which you will find in practically any hymnal
you pick up, but also in his other works. He is one of the most
deeply devotional of English poets.

1.   . . . he raised the knife;
God saw and said, "Forbear!
Yon ram shall yield his meaner life:
Behold the victim there."

What Bible incident is referred to?

2.   The scape-goat on his head
The people's trespass bore,
And to the desert led,
Was to be seen no more.

You have often heard the term "scape-goat." Do you know how
it originated?

3.   When Moses stood with arms spread wide,
Success was found on Israel's side.

Explain the allusion.

4.   . . . Gideon's fleece, which drenched with dew he found
While moisture none refreshed the herbs around. . . .

How did Gideon use this fleece?

5.   Elisha's eye, that when Gehazi strayed,
Went with him and saw all the game he played.

When did Elisha's eye follow Gehazi thus?

[Answers on page 118]

No. 5. THE BIBLE AND BYRON

No one thinks of Byron as a religious poet, yet among his first works was *Hebrew Melodies* and among his last the drama of *Cain*.

1.   Oh, God! receive thy servant and
           Forgive his slayer, for he knew not what
           He did.

These words are put into the mouth of Abel. They are quoted from whom?

2.   The buried prophet answered to the hag
                   Of Endor.

Who was " the buried prophet " ?

3.   The harp the monarch minstrel swept. . . .

Who was " the monarch minstrel " ?

4.   " Let the men of lore appear
           The wisest of the earth,
           And expound the words of fear,
           That mar our royal mirth."

What king gives this order?

5.   A man shall say to a man, " Believe in me,
           And walk the waters," and the man shall walk
           The billows and be safe.

What incident is referred to?

No. 6. THE BIBLE AND TENNYSON

1.   And marked me, even as Cain.

Why was Cain marked?

2.   But in the darkness and the cloud
           As over Sinai's peaks of old
           While Israel made their gods of gold. . . .

Of what story are we reminded?

110   [Answers on page 118]

3.   That God would move
          And strike the hard, hard rock, and thence,
          Sweet in their utmost bitterness,
          Would issue tears of penitence.

Explain the allusion.

4.   The church on Peter's rock.

Why on Peter's rock?

5.   My sin was as a thorn
          Among the thorns that girt thy brow.

Explain the allusion.

No. 7. THE BIBLE AND BROWNING

1.   Where he stands in the shadow with his knife,
      Waiting to see what Delilah will do.

Who was Delilah?

2.   So a fool
      Once touched the ark—poor Uzzah, that am I!

What befell Uzzah as a result of his touching the ark?

3.   Was not the son of Jesse ruddy, sleek,
           Pleasant to look on, pleasant every way?

Is the description accurate?

4.   " Give me the man," I say with him of Gath,
      " That we may fight together."

Who was " him of Gath " ?

5.   Like to Ahasuerus, that shrewd prince,
           I will begin . . . and read a history.

Who was Ahasuerus?

6.   As if the quesy river could not hold
      Its swallowed Jonas, but discharged the meal.

Explain the reference.

[Answers on pages 118–119]   111

7.   She sought for aid; and if she made mistake
I' the man could aid most, why—so mortals do:
Even the blessed Magdalen mistook
Far less forgivably.

Whom did the blessed Magdalen mistake?

8.   How one brought up at the very feet of law,
As I, awaits the grave Gamaliel's nod.

Who was Gamaliel?

9.   I plucked the absolute dead from God's own bar,
And raised up Dorcas . . .

Who was Dorcas?

10.   Saint Paul has had enough, and to spare, I trow,
Of ragged, runaway Onesimus.

Who was Onesimus?

No. 8. THE BIBLE AND MATTHEW ARNOLD

1.   . . . as Moses felt,
When he lay in the night by his flock
On the starlit Arabian waste?

When did Moses ever keep flocks in Arabia?

2.   No jot, no tittle, from the law shall pass
Till all have been fulfilled.

Who is quoted?

3.   " He saves the sheep, the goats he cannot save,"
So rang Tertullian's sentence. . . .

Explain the allusion.

4.   That nailed, thorn-crowned man . . .

He means of course—whom?

5.   But was it thou—I think
Surely it was!—that bard

112   [Answers on page 119]

Unnamed, who, Goethe said,
Had every other gift but wanted Love.

What did Paul say about having other gifts and wanting love?

No. 9. THE BIBLE AND KIPLING

1.   Why brought ye us from bondage,
        Our loved Egyptian night?

Who complained in this fashion to whom?

2. One of Kipling's poems, *A School Song,* begins

        Let us now praise famous men.

Did he find these words in the Bible?

3. The sons of Mary seldom bother, for they have inherited
        that good part,
    But the sons of Martha favor their mother, of the careful
        soul and the troubled heart,
    And because she lost her temper once and because she was
        rude to the Lord her guest,
    Her sons must wait upon Mary's sons—world without end,
        reprieve or rest.

When was Martha " rude to the Lord her guest " ?

4.   Surely in toil or fray
            Under an alien sky,
            Comfort it is to say,
            " Of no mean city am I."

Whom is he quoting?

5.   So we wrestled wi' Apollyon. . . .

Is Apollyon mentioned in the Bible?

No. 10. THE BIBLE AND MASEFIELD

1. An' that there haughty albatross cruisin' round—
        Belike he's Admiral Nelson or Admiral Noah.

Why " Admiral " Noah?

[Answers on pages 119–120]   113

2. A 'Lijah in a fiery car. . . .

What event is referred to?

3. Quinquereme of Nineveh from distant Ophir,
Rowing home to haven in sunny Palestine,
With a cargo of ivory,
And apes and peacocks. . . .

Is this cargo according to the Bible, or is the poet drawing upon his imagination?

4. Ah me, I thought, how many, many times
Genius thus slumbers in a human soul,
Waiting as Lazarus waited, for a voice. . . .

Lazarus waited—where?

5. Masefield makes one of his characters say:

The English church both is and was
A subsidy of Caiaphas.

Who was Caiaphas?

No. 11. THE BIBLE AND WHITTIER

1. My Gerizim and Ebal
Are in each human soul.
The still, small voice of blessing,
And Sinai's thunder roll.

What is meant by Gerizim and Ebal?

2. Yet one knelt not; stark, gaunt and blind,
His arms the massive pillars twined—
An eyeless captive, strong with hate,
He stood there like an evil Fate.

Who is described?

3. And the chariots of Jabin rolled harmlessly on
For the arm of the Lord was Abinoam's son.

Who was Abinoam's son?

4. Well! He who fashioned Peter's dream,
To bless them all is able;

114

[Answers on page 120]

And bird and beast and creeping thing
Make clean upon his table.

What dream of Peter's was this?

5   Not unto manhood's heart alone
    The holy influence steals;
   Warm with a rapture not its own,
    The heart of woman feels!
   As she who by Samaria's wall
    The Savior's errand sought—
   Or those who with the fervent Paul
    And meek Aquila wrought.

What woman " wrought " with Paul and Aquila?

No. 12. THE BIBLE AND LOWELL

1. And rattle away till he's old as Methusalem,
  At the head of a march to the last new Jerusalem.

Why is Methuselah so often cited as an example of a very old man?

2. " Sing now and make your voices heard in hymns of
   praise," cried he,
  " As did the Israelites of old, safe walking through the
   sea."

When did the Israelites walk safely through the sea?

3.   If thou hast wandered in the wilderness
   And findest not Sinai, 'tis thy soul is poor.

To what is the reference?

4. With every anguish of our earthly part
  The spirit's path grows clearer; this was meant
  When Jesus touched the blind man's lids with clay.

Go on with the story. The man had a part in his own healing.
Jesus told him to do—what?

5.   . . . he girt his young life up in gilded mail
   And set forth in search of the Holy Grail.

[Answers on pages 120–121]

Many English poets have written of the search for the Grail. What was it?

No. 13.   THE BIBLE AND LONGFELLOW

1.   Hold the fleet angel fast until he bless thee.

What is the story referred to?

2.   Beware! The Israelite of old who tore
             The lion in his path . . .

Who was this " Israelite of old " ?

3.   Like as Elias in heaven, when he cast off from him his
     mantle.

When did this happen and by whom was it witnessed?

4.   Let him not boast who puts his armor on
        As he who puts it off, the battle done.

Whom is the poet quoting?

5.   Like the prophetic voice that cried,
             To John in Patmos, " Write! "

What did he write?

ANSWERS

SECTION VI

THE BIBLE AND THE POETS

No. 1. THE BIBLE AND CHAUCER

1. First to the chief butler and chief baker. Later to Pharaoh. Gen. 40 and 41.
2. Samson. Judges 16.
3. Because of his tactless rudeness to David. I Sam. **25.**
4. King Nebuchadnezzar. Dan. 4.
5. Pilate. John 18: 38.

No. 2. THE BIBLE AND SHAKESPEARE

1. Though she bore a son to Abraham, it was not through this son that Shylock's people traced their descent. Gen. **21.**
2. Jael and Sisera. Judges 4.
3. Gaza. Judges 16.
4. "How art thou fallen from heaven, O Lucifer, son of the morning . . ." (And the verses following.) Isa. 14: 12.
5. The massacre of the innocents. Matt. 2: 16–18.
6. He did. Matt. 4: 5–6.
7. That of the Prodigal Son.
8. The healing of the possessed man, who said that his name was Legion. Luke 8.
9. The robber, whom the Jews demanded of Pilate in place of Jesus. John 18: 40.
10. Because it was by a kiss that Judas betrayed his Master. Matt. 26.

No. 3. THE BIBLE AND MILTON

1. "He was the father of all such as handle the harp . . ." Gen. 4: 21.

2. Dagon. I Sam. 5.

3. The wise men who came to pay homage to the new-born Christ.

4. Christ's temptation in the wilderness. Matt. 4.

5. Peter. Matt. 16: 19.

No. 4. THE BIBLE AND COWPER

1. Abraham's sacrifice of Isaac. Gen. 22.

2. The priest, in a solemn ceremony, transferred the sins of the people to a goat, which was then sent into the wilderness. Lev. 16: 21.

3. In a battle between Israel and Amalek, the Israelites " prevailed " so long as Moses held up his hands in supplication. Ex. 17: 11–12.

4. He used it as a sign by which to test the genuineness of his call to lead the armies of Israel. Judges 6.

5. When his cupidity led him to follow Naaman the Syrian. II Kings 5.

No. 5. THE BIBLE AND BYRON

1. From Christ—on the cross. Luke 23: 34.

2. Samuel. I Sam. 28.

3. King David.

4. Belshazzar. Daniel 5.

5. Christ's walking upon the water and bidding Peter come to him. Matt. 14: 25.

No. 6. THE BIBLE AND TENNYSON

1. Not because of his crime but to protect him from the vengeance of fellow men. Gen. 4: 15.

2. Of how, while Moses was receiving the law upon Mount Sinai, the people made a golden calf. Ex. 32.

3. The incident referred to is that of the water coming from the rock, when struck by Moses. Num. 20.

4. Jesus said to him (Matt. 16: 18) " thou art Peter, and upon this rock will I build my church."

118

5. The allusion is to the crown of thorns which the soldiers placed upon the head of Christ in mockery. Matt. 27: 29.

No. 7. THE BIBLE AND BROWNING

1. The Philistine woman who betrayed Samson to his enemies.
2. II Sam. 6: 7 says: " God smote him there for his error and there he died by the ark of God."
3. It is. I Sam. 16: 12 says, " he was ruddy, and withal of a beautiful countenance and goodly to look upon."
4. Goliath. The words are a part of his challenge to the army of King Saul.
5. The king named in the book of Esther, who reigned over " an hundred and seven and twenty provinces." As to the " history " which he read, see chapter 6.
6. Jonah, chapter 2, tells how the prophet was cast out by " the great fish," upon the dry land.
7. The risen Savior, " supposing him to be the gardener." John 20: 15.
8. A famous teacher of the Jewish law. Saul of Tarsus was the most famous of his pupils.
9. The good woman whom Peter (Acts 9) raised from the dead.
10. The runaway slave for whom Paul speaks in his letter to Philemon.

No. 8. THE BIBLE AND MATTHEW ARNOLD

1. When he fled from the wrath of Pharaoh into Midian. Ex. 2.
2. Jesus. Matt. 5: 18.
3. It refers to Jesus' picture of the Last Judgment, where there shall be a separation, " as a shepherd divideth his sheep from the goats." Matt. 25: 32.
4. Jesus.
5. " Though I have . . ." (He enumerates many gifts.) ". . . and have not love, I am nothing." I Cor. 13.

No. 9. THE BIBLE AND KIPLING

1. The children of Israel to Moses, who had led them out of slavery. Ex. 16: 2–3.
2. Not in the Bible as most of us know it. The words are found in the Apocrypha (Ecclesiasticus 44: 1) which in many old Bibles is printed between the Old and New Testaments.
3. When she came to him to complain of her sister, who had left her to " serve alone." Luke 10: 39–42.
4. Paul. Acts 21: 39.
5. Once, in Rev. 9: 11. We know him chiefly as a character in Bunyan's " Pilgrim's Progress."

No. 10. THE BIBLE AND MASEFIELD

1. Presumably because the speaker thought of him as commanding the only " navy " then afloat.
2. The translation of Elijah. II Kings 2.
3. The Bible confirms it. I Kings 10: 22.
4. In the tomb at Bethany.
5. The high priest before whom Jesus was condemned.

No. 11. THE BIBLE AND WHITTIER

1. They were the mountains of blessing and cursing. Deut. 27.
2. Samson. Judges 16.
3. Barak: the general who led Israel's armies under Deborah. Judges 4.
4. That which came to him just before he received his invitation to visit Cornelius. Acts 10.
5. Priscilla. Acts 18: 2–4.

No. 12. THE BIBLE AND LOWELL

1. His age is the greatest of any man mentioned in the Bible —969 years.
2. When they fled from Egypt, pursued by Pharaoh's army.
3. To the wanderings of Israel in the wilderness and to the law given them by God from Sinai.

120

4. " Go and wash in the pool of Siloam." John 9: 7.

5. The cup from which Christ and his apostles are supposed to have drunk the wine at the Last Supper. (Some archeologists would identify it with the recently discovered Great Chalice of Antioch.)

No. 13. THE BIBLE AND LONGFELLOW

1. That of the angel which wrestled with Jacob. Gen. 32.

2. Samson. Judges 14.

3. It happened in Elijah's translation and was witnessed by Elisha. II Kings 2.

4. The words are those of King Ahab to Benhadad. I Kings 20: 11.

5. The book of Revelation.

MISCELLANEOUS QUIZZES
"STORIES ABOUT . . ."
No. 1

An American novelist, whom you would quite probably recognize were I to name her, sometimes told stories to a group of children whom she knew well, doing it in this fashion:

"What shall I tell you about today?" she would ask.

"A turtle," one child would say.

"A broken hand organ," another would suggest.

"A cocoanut."

"A wheelbarrow."

And her task was to put into *one story* the three, or four, or half dozen things they named. That, it seems to me, might be pretty hard. But, to one who knows the Bible well, it should not be difficult to combine the things named below, for these stories do not need to be "made up," they are right there in the Bible, needing only to be remembered.

1. A dove. A raven. A boat. A rainbow.

2. A knife. A load of wood. A ram. A thicket.

3. A bow and arrows. A blind man. A boy who put on his brother's clothes.

4. A fine coat. A dry pit. Two dreams. A seventeen-year-old boy.

5. A food shortage. A long journey. Spies? Refunded money.

6. Flies. Lice. Frogs. Hail and a number of other unpleasant things.

7. Some stalks of flax. Three days' hiding. A scarlet thread in a window.

8. Seven priests. Seven horns. Seven days. A great shout. A captured city.

9. Soldiers. Lamps. Trumpets. Broken pitchers.

10. A bees' nest. A wedding. A fight with a lion.

[Answers on page 134]

No. 2

1. A battle. A bad promise. Some honey on a stick.
2. A crown prince and his " orderly." Two sharp rocks. A half acre battlefield.
3. A runner with earth on his head. A blind man ninety-eight years old. Departed glory.
4. A mule. An oak tree. Three darts. A great pit.
5. A royal visit. A camel train. Spices. Precious stones.
6. A fire. An earthquake. A high wind. A cave.
7. A little girl. A sick army officer. Ten suits of clothes. (The Bible calls them " changes of raiment.")
8. Cheap food. Four lepers. A deserted camp. A man trampled to death.
9. A sleepless king. A history book. The king's horse. The king's clothes. A triumphal procession.
10. A tall tree. The tree's stump. A dream. A king who ate grass.

No. 3

1. A baby. Tax collecting. A crowded inn. A stable.
2. A ship. A storm. A man asleep. A great calm.
3. A place of tombs. A herd of pigs. A crazy man.
4. A prison. A birthday party. A girl who danced.
5. Two fish. Five loaves of bread. Twelve baskets.
6. A well. A tired and thirsty traveller. An astonished woman. A two days' stay with " foreigners."
7. Two servant girls. A rooster. A man who swore.
8. Three women. Sunrise. Sweet spices. A great stone.
9. An upper chamber. Weeping widows. Home-made coats.
10. A snake. A shipwreck. A bonfire.

No. 4

The articles or persons named should suggest stories which Jesus told.
1. A banquet. Ten oxen. Some lame and blind men.
2. Thorns. Birds. Seeds. A rock.

[Answers on pages 134–135]

3. Big crops. Torn-down barns. A man who wanted to be happy but wasn't.

4. Some money. A long trip. A napkin.

5. An unexpected guest. A sleepy man. Three loaves of bread.

6. A dog. A beggar. Some angels.

7. A hedge. A tower. An order for fruit. A crime.

8. Ten girls. A wedding. An oil shortage.

9. A market place. Men who wanted a job. A complaint about wages.

10. A calf. Some pigs. Music and dancing.

TRUE OR FALSE?

No. 1

1. The first five books of the Bible, often called the " Books of Moses," were really written by him.

2. Adam and Eve had only two children—Cain and Abel.

3. In the story of the flood, we are told that Noah took into the ark with him two animals of a kind.

4. Though Abraham is counted as a man of peace, he once led into battle a larger number of fighting men than Gideon commanded when he won his greatest victory.

5. Of the three patriarchs, Abraham, Isaac and Jacob, two visited Egypt.

6. Each of the 12 tribes of Israel is named after one of the sons of Jacob.

7. After Pharaoh's host was overwhelmed in the Red Sea, the Egyptians made no further attempt to prevent the exodus of the Israelites.

8. On the death of Moses, the people met and elected Joshua as his successor.

9. The books of Kings and Chronicles cover much the same ground but from different points of view.

10. The Jewish state was one of the Great Powers of the ancient world.

     [Answers on pages 135–136]

No. 2

1. Solomon, King David's successor, was the son of Bath-sheba, once the wife of Uriah the Hittite.

2. Even after the revolt of the ten tribes, the people of the northern kingdom continued to come to Jerusalem to worship.

3. In the time of the kings, Israel had no educational system for the training of religious leaders.

4. The seventy years' captivity of Israel does not mean that all of the people were carried into captivity.

5. The return from captivity was accomplished in the face of bitter opposition from the authorities.

6. When his call first came to him, Isaiah, like Moses, felt himself utterly unequal to it and asked to be released from its responsibility.

7. Baruch was the friend and loyal secretary of the prophet Isaiah.

8. " The dream I dreamed last night I have forgotten: but tell it to me and explain it, or I will put all of you to death." The Bible has a story of a king who said just about this to a group of his servants.

9. Among the most scathing and eloquent of all who have ever denounced the oppression of the poor stands the prophet Amos.

10. The preaching of Jonah in Nineveh accomplished the purpose for which he was sent there.

No. 3

1. The four gospels were not all written by members of Jesus' inner group—the twelve.

2. The order of books in the New Testament, Matthew, Mark, Luke, etc., does not indicate the order in which they were written.

3. When the Wise Men came to Jerusalem, asking, " Where is he that is born king of the Jews? " the chief priests and scribes were puzzled and did not know what to tell them.

4. A belief prevailed in Jesus' time that the appearance of the Messiah must be preceded by the coming of the prophet Elijah.

[Answers on pages 136–137]

5. Jesus himself never endorsed this belief.

6. Even the Samaritans shared the prevailing belief in the coming of a Messiah.

7. John the Baptist, while popular with the common people, was invariably denounced by the religious leaders of the time.

8. Through all his persecutions and imprisonment, John the Baptist never questioned that Jesus was the promised Messiah.

9. Jesus was scrupulously careful about the people with whom he associated.

10. While his closest associates were poor and unlearned men, Jesus had some friends among the wealthy and educated.

PICK YOUR ANSWERS

No. 1

1. The twelve tribes of Israel, as commonly listed, comprise the following: Reuben, Simeon, Ephraim, Judah, Issachar, Manassseh, Gad, Asher, Benjamin, Dan, Naphtali, Zebulun. Two are named for sons of Joseph—not Jacob. Which two?

2. One of the sons of Jacob became the ancestor of the hereditary Jewish priesthood. His name was—

Benjamin? Judah? Levi? Naphtali? Simeon?

3. The mountain upon which Moses received the tables of the law was Mount—

Horeb? Nebo? Gilboa? Sinai? Ebal?

4. All through their desert wanderings, the Israelites carried with them, as their most precious religious possession, the ark of the covenant. It was not appropriately housed until the reign of—

David? Solomon? Josiah? Jeroboam? Herod the Great?

5. The spectacular victory of Gideon and his 300 was won over the—

Ammonites? Jebusites? Philistines? Midianites?

126   [Answers on page 137]

6. We are told that one of the judges over Israel married a Philistine woman. This judge was—

Jotham? Gideon? Samson? Jephtha? Abimelech?

7. The mother of the prophet Samuel, who in his childhood had " lent him to the Lord," bore the still familiar name of—

Rachel? Hulda? Deborah? Hannah? Miriam? Joanna?

8. In the days of Eli and Samuel, the center of the Jewish religious worship was—

Shiloh? Hebron? Shechem? Gilgal?

9. When David went out to do battle with Goliath, he was armed with—

A bow and arrows?
A sling and five smooth stones?
The personal weapons of King Saul?

10. During the reigns of both Saul and David, the most dangerous and persistent of Israel's enemies were—

The Ammonites? Hittites? Philistines? Phoenicians?

No. 2

1. The life of King Saul came to a dramatic close when—

He was assassinated by a treacherous follower?
Fell upon his own sword?
Was slain by his armor-bearer, whom he commanded to kill him, rather than permit him to be taken prisoner?

2. David seems to have felt no compunction for contriving the treacherous murder of Uriah the Hittite until rebuked by the prophet—

Gad? Ahijah? Nathan? Samuel? Joel?

3. Throughout David's reign, his troops were commanded by a strong, loyal but often ruthless soldier named—

Abner? Abishai? Joab? Phineas?

[Answers on page 137]

4. Solomon's succession to the throne was contested by his brother—

Absalom? Adonijah? Amnon? Jedediah?

5. An alliance advantageous politically but disastrous religiously was made by King Solomon, when he married the daughter of the king of—

Tyre? Babylon? Syria? Egypt? Sheba?

6. When the ten tribes revolted, after the death of Solomon, they established their capital at—

Jezreel? Dothan? Samaria? Damascus?

7. In I Kings 19, we read that, when Elijah fled from Queen Jezebel, he went a forty days journey to Mount—

Tabor? Lebanon? Carmel? Horeb?

8. The kings of Israel frequently tried to usurp the offices of the priests. One king, punished for such an attempt, was—

Josiah? Jereboam? Uzziah? Zedekiah? Ahab?

9. After their seventy years of captivity, the Jews were permitted to return to their homeland by the king of—

Egypt? Babylonia? Nineveh? Persia?

10. The words of Handel's great *Messiah* chorus, " For unto us a child is born," are found in the book of the prophet—

Ezekiel? Jeremiah? Malachi? Isaiah? Habakkuk?

No. 3

1. Jonah, seeking to " flee from the presence of the Lord," took ship at—

Tyre? Tarshish? Zidon? Joppa?

2. Not only was Jesus born in Bethlehem, it was also the birthplace of—

Saul? Jeremiah? David? Samuel? John the Baptist?

                    [Answers on pages 137–138]

3. The people of Jesus' time had reason for their belief in the return to earth of the prophet Elijah, since this had been foretold by the prophet—

Isaiah? Hosea? Jeremiah? Malachi? Joel?

4. Herod had no love for John the Baptist, but when he finally gave orders for his execution he did it only because—

He was intoxicated?
His wife had threatened him?
He had made a rash promise and was ashamed to take it back?

5. The greatest sermon of all time was preached—

In the courts of the temple at Jerusalem?
From a borrowed boat?
On a mountain top?
Near the pool of Siloam?

6. When Jesus had cured the demoniac, who said that his name was Legion, he commanded him—

To tell no man?
To go and show himself to the priests?
To return to his own home as an evidence of what God had done for him?

7. So far as we know, only one of the twelve apostles ever held any public office. He was—

Peter? Judas? John? Matthew? Bartholomew?

8. In Matthew 17 we read that Jesus, taking with him three of the apostles, went up into a high mountain and was transfigured before them. Which three did he take?

(The names of the twelve, as given in Matthew 10, are: Simon Peter, Andrew, James, John, Philip, Bartholomew, Thomas, Matthew, James the son of Alphaeus, Lebbaeus surnamed Thaddaeus, Simon the Canaanite and Judas Iscariot.)

9. The above list of apostles contains two pairs of brothers. They were—

[Answers on page 138]   **129**

10. A third, perhaps more, of the apostles earned their living by—

Farming? Weaving? As potters? As day laborers? Fishermen?

No. 4

1. The apostle sometimes referred to as " the doubter " was named—

Andrew? Philip? Thomas? James? Simon the Canaanite?

2. You have heard the story of how, in order to catch a glimpse of Jesus, Zacchaeus ran ahead and climbed up into a tree. As to kind of tree, you may have forgotten that it was—

An oak? A pine? A sycamore? A fir? A cedar?

3. The first person to see Jesus after his resurrection was—

Peter? Cleopas? John? Mary Magdalene? Mary the mother of James and Joses?

4. When Paul was in Damascus, immediately after his conversion, his sight, lost to him for a time, was restored through the prayer of a disciple named—

Jonas? Epaphroditus? Stephanas? Ananias? Aquila?

5. Coming to Joppa, in search of Peter, the servants of Cornelius found him, as they had been told they would, in the home of a man named Simon, who lived by the seaside and earned his living as a—

Fisherman? Soldier? Tax collector? Potter? Musician? Tanner?

6. When the church at Antioch sent out its first foreign missionaries, one was Paul. The other was—

Silas? Barnabas? John Mark? Timothy?

7. Paul's journeys carried him farther than you might imagine. Indeed he is supposed to have visited all of the following countries excepting one. The exception is—

Italy? Greece? Egypt? Macedonia? Spain? Arabia?

130   [Answers on page 138]

8. A plan which Paul and Barnabas had formed for making a missionary journey together and visiting churches they had already established was given up because of their difference over a fellow worker. This man was—

Timothy? Silas? John Mark? Philip? Luke?

9. The number of Paul's missionary journeys, described in the book of Acts, is—

Two? Five? Three? Seven?

10. All but two of the following New Testament epistles bear the names of the writers, not the addressees. The two exceptions are—

I and II Peter? I, II and III John? Jude?
I and II Timothy? James?

No. 5

1. Here are the names of six men and six women. Each of the women was mother of one of the men. Can you sort them out correctly?

The women: Sarah, Rachel, Elisabeth, Rebekah, Bathsheba, Eunice.

The men: John the Baptist, Solomon, Timothy, Isaac, Jacob, Joseph.

2. Sort out the following brothers and sisters:

Asahel, Mary, Lazarus, Abishai, Martha, Joab.

3. Of the following, four were priests, four soldiers. Which are which?

Aaron, Abner, Abiathar, Claudius Lysias,
Cornelius, Eli, Joab, Nadab.

4. Four of the following were kings, *five* were prophets. Which are which—and how do you explain it?

Ahijah, Ahaz, Agabus, Nathan, Zimri,
Zechariah, Nahun, Joash.

5. Here are the names of seven men, one woman and eight

callings. (Not all can be called trades.) How near can you come to attaching the right callings to the right persons? Lydia, Peter, Demetrius, Nimrod, Luke, Matthew, Joseph—the New Testament Joseph, Barabbas. Fisherman, hunter, silversmith, tax collector, carpenter, robber, doctor, " seller of purple."

6. In Canaan the Israelites were surrounded by many hostile tribes and groups, with all of whom, at one time or another, they seem to have been at war. Among the following seven groups however is one with which they were never at war. Which one is it?

Midianites? Jebusites? Amalekites? Ammonites?
Perrizites? Nazirites? Hittites?

7. Surrounded by these people of other blood, the Israelites had, as one would expect, many contacts pleasant and otherwise with individual aliens. Here are six tribal (or city) names and the names of six persons. Can you sort them up properly?

The persons: Doeg, Ruth, Uriah, Delilah, Obed-edom, Agag.
The designations: Amalekite, Edomite, Gittite, Hittite, Moabitess, Philistine.

8. Four of these men were friends of Jesus: the others were friends of the Christian movement but probably never saw its founder. Which are which?

James, Barnabas, Nathanael, Stephen, Apollos,
Silas, Peter, Lazarus.

9. Five of these men held positions of one sort or another under the Roman government. One did not. Which one?

Pilate? Felix? Festus? Cleopas? Cornelius?
Claudius Lysias?

10. Three of these were sons of the other three. How do they sort up?

Abraham, Seth, Jacob, Adam, Ishmael, Benjamin.

　　　　　　　　　　　　　[Answers on page 139]

COMPARISONS OF THE LIVES OF JESUS
No. 1

As one would expect, the four men who wrote biographies of Jesus had each his individual point of view. All did not record exactly the same facts or record them in exactly the same way. Also, quite possibly one (or two) of them knew of an earlier life of Jesus and Luke or John may have said, " I don't need to put that in: Mark has already told about it." Or, " I better put that in: I see Mark has left it out."

The average Bible reader however seldom makes the kind of comparison that the following questions suggest.

1. Mary's beautiful hymn of praise, beginning " My soul doth magnify the Lord," (the so-called *Magnificat*) is found in but one of the gospels. Which one?

2. Which gospel tells of the coming of the wise men and which of the shepherds?

3. Some mention of John the Baptist is found in all four of the lives of Jesus. Is this statement true or false?

4. Concerning Jesus' teaching of the multitudes, we read, " without a parable spake he not unto them." Yet one gospel records not a single parable. Which one?

5. Jesus is often described as curing leprosy, yet in one of the gospels the word leper does not once occur. Which one?

6. Jesus himself seemed often to regard his miracles of healing as of secondary importance. Perhaps for this reason one of the gospels has no mention of any miracle of healing. True or false?

7. In all four of the gospels, much space is given to telling of the last supper of Jesus with the disciples. True or false?

8. How many of the gospels give circumstantial accounts of the resurrection?

9. One of the most beautiful of New Testament stories is that of the two disciples on their way to Emmaus, who fell into conversation with the risen Christ, though " their eyes were holden that they should not know him." We read this in how many of the gospels?

10. Would you say that the ascension is recorded in one, two or three of the gospels?

[Answers on pages 139–140]

ANSWERS

MISCELLANEOUS QUIZZES

"STORIES ABOUT . . ."

No. 1

1. The story is that of the ending of the flood. Gen. 8 and 9.
2. Abraham's sacrifice of Isaac: how he was taught that human sacrifice (practiced by the peoples about him) was not the right way in which to worship God. Gen. 22.
3. Isaac's blessing of Jacob. Gen. 27.
4. Joseph sold into slavery. Gen. 37.
5. Joseph's brothers on their first visit to Egypt. Gen. 42.
6. The plagues of Egypt. Ex. 8, 9 and 10.
7. The adventure of the spies in Jericho. Joshua 2.
8. The siege of Jericho. Joshua 6.
9. The victory of Gideon and his three hundred. Judges 7.
10. One of the exploits of Samson. Judges 14.

No. 2

1. Saul's rash vow and Jonathan's imminent danger of being sacrificed. I Sam. 14.
2. The victory of Jonathan and his armor bearer over the Philistines at Michmash. I Sam. 14.
3. Defeat of the Israelites and the death of Eli. I Sam. 4.
4. The death of Abalsom. II Sam. 18.
5. The visit of the Queen of Sheba to Solomon. I Kings 10.
6. Elijah at Horeb. I Kings 19.
7. The healing of Naaman the Syrian. II Kings 5.
8. The dramatic raising of the siege of Samaria. II Kings 7.
9. The honor shown by the king to Mordecai. Esther 6.
10. Nebuchadnezzar's dream and the punishment of his pride. Dan. 4.

No. 3

1. The birth of Jesus. Luke 2.
2. Jesus stilling the tempest. Mark 4.
3. The healing of the demoniac who called himself Legion. Mark 5.
4. The death of John the Baptist. Mark 6.
5. The feeding of the five thousand. Matt. 14.
6. The talk with the woman of Sychar. John 4.
7. Peter's denial of his Master. Matt. 26.
8. The coming of the women to the empty tomb on Easter morning. Mark 16.
9. The raising of Dorcas. Acts 9.
10. Paul's shipwreck upon the island of Melita. Acts 28.

No. 4

1. The Parable of the Great Supper. Luke 14.
2. The Parable of the Sower. Luke 8.
3. The Parable of the Rich Fool. Luke 12.
4. The Parable of the Talents. Matt. 25.
5. The Parable of the Friend at Midnight. Luke 11.
6. The Rich Man and Lazarus. Luke 16.
7. The Parable of the Wicked Husbandmen. Matt. 21.
8. The Parable of the Ten Virgins. Matt. 25.
9. The Parable of the Laborers in the Vineyard. Matt. 20.
10. The Parable of the Prodigal Son. Luke 15.

TRUE OR FALSE?

No. 1

1. False: at least that is not the view of modern scholarship; nor does the Bible anywhere state that Moses wrote all these books.
2. False: Gen. 5: 4 speaks of " sons and daughters."
3. False: of some animals he took seven. Gen. 7: 2.
4. True: in Genesis 14 we read of his victory over " four kings."
5. True. Abraham (Gen. 12: 10–20), as well as Jacob, went to Egypt in a time of famine.

6. False: Ephraim and Manasses were not sons of Jacob.

7. True: see Ex. 14.

8. False: Joshua was appointed to his position by Moses. Deut. 34: 9.

9. True: as even a superficial comparison of the books will show.

10. False. It depends of course on the meaning one gives to the word " great " but Israel was never a " great power " in the sense that Assyria, Babylonia and Egypt were.

No. 2

1. True: see I Kings 2: 13.

2. False: Jeroboam, king of the northern kingdom, almost immediately established centers of worship within his own borders. I Kings 12: 28–29.

3. False: at least the Sons of the Prophets (II Kings 2) would seem to have been receiving specialized religious instruction.

4. True: " the poorest sort of the people of the land " were left in possession. II Kings 24: 14 and 25: 12.

5. False: the return of the exiles had official encouragement. Ezra 1.

6. False: his answer was, " Here am I: send me." Isa. 6: 7–8.

7. False: he held this relation to the prophet Jeremiah.

8. True: the story goes on to tell how the prophet Daniel met the crisis. Dan. 2.

9. True: to fully appreciate it, one should read all nine chapters of his book.

10. True: the narrative declares that the Ninevites repented and believed God. Jonah 3: 5.

No. 3

1. True: neither Luke nor Mark are named as among the twelve.

2. True: practically all scholars are agreed that some of the epistles were written before any of the gospels.

3. False: they knew exactly what to tell them. Matt. **2.**

4. True: such was the teaching of the scribes. Matt. **17: 10.**

5. False: he said that, in effect, Elijah had already come and " they knew him not." Matt. **17: 12.**

6. True: the Samaritan woman, with whom Jesus talked beside Jacob's well, spoke of it as something universally accepted. John **4: 25.**

7. False: the religious leaders, whatever they may have thought of John, were very careful as to what they said about him. Matt. **21: 25.**

8. False: he once sent to Jesus to inquire, " Art thou he that should come or do we look for another? "

9. False: he went to those who needed him, apparently quite indifferent to criticism. Matt. **9: 11.**

10. True: Zacchaeus, Joseph of Arimathea and Nicodemus are examples.

PICK YOUR ANSWERS

No. 1

1. Ephraim and Manasseh. Gen. **48: 1.**
2. Levi.
3. The mountain upon which Moses received the tables of the law was known as both Horeb and Sinai.
4. Solomon.
5. The Midianites—assisted by the Amalekites. Judges **7.**
6. Samson. Judges **14.**
7. Hannah. I Sam. **1.**
8. Shiloh. I Sam. **1: 3.**
9. A sling and five smooth stones. I Sam. **17: 40.**
10. The Philistines.

No. 2

1. He fell upon his own sword. I Sam. **31.**
2. Nathan. II Sam. **12.**
3. Joab.
4. Adonijah. I Kings **1.**

5. Egypt. I Kings 3.
6. Samaria.
7. Horeb.
8. Uzziah. II Chron. 26.
9. Persia. Ezra 1: 1.
10. Isaiah 9: 6.

No. 3

1. Joppa. Jonah 1: 3.
2. David.
3. Malachi 4: 5.
4. He was ashamed to take back his rash promise. Matt. 14: 9.
5. On a mountain top. Matt. 5: 1.
6. To return to his own house, as an evidence of what God had done for him. Luke 8: 38–39.
7. Matthew. Matt. 10: 3.
8. Peter, James and John. Matt. 17: 1–2.
9. Peter and Andrew. James and John.
10. Fishing.

No. 4

1. Thomas. John 20: 24–25.
2. A sycamore. Luke 19: 4.
3. Mary Magdalene. Mark 16: 9.
4. Ananias. Acts 9.
5. Tanner. Acts 10.
6. Barnabas. Acts 13: 2.
7. Egypt.
8. John Mark. Acts 15: 36–39.
9. Three.
10. I and II Timothy.

No. 5

1. Sarah was the mother of Isaac.
   Rachel the mother of Joseph.
   Elisabeth the mother of John the Baptist.

Rebekah the mother of Jacob.
Bathsheba the mother of Solomon.
Eunice the mother of Timothy.

2. Asahel, Abishai and Joab were brothers.
Mary, Martha and Lazarus were sisters and brother.

3. The four priests were: Aaron, Abiathar, Eli and Nadab.
The four soldiers were: Abner, Claudius, Lysias, Cornelius and Joab.

4. The four kings were: Ahaz, Zimri, Zechariah and Joash.
The *five* prophets were: Ahijah, Agabus, Nathan, Zechariah and Nahun. (The Bible mentions one Zechariah who was a king and another who was a prophet.)

5. Simon Peter was a fisherman.
Nimrod a hunter.   Barabbas a robber.
Demetrius a silversmith.   Luke a doctor.
Matthew a tax collector.   Lydia a " seller of purple."
Joseph a carpenter.

6. The Nazirites. These were not a tribe but a group (Numbers 6) of " individuals under a personal vow."

7. Doeg the Edomite.
Ruth the Moabitess.
Uriah the Hittite.
Delilah a Philistine.
Obed-edom the Gittite.
Agag the Amalekite.

8. Friends of Jesus: James, Peter, Lazarus, Nathanael.
Friends of the Christian movement: Barnabas, Silas, Stephen, Apollos.

9. Cleopas.

10. Ishmael was the son of Abraham.
Seth the son of Adam.
Benjamin was the son of Jacob.

COMPARISONS OF THE LIVES OF JESUS

No. 1

1. Luke 1.
2. Matthew tells of the wise men. Luke tells of the shepherds. Mark and John tell almost nothing of Jesus' birth.

3. True.

4. The Gospel of John.

5. Again the Gospel of John.

6. False: miracles of healing are mentioned by all the gospel writers.

7. True: the fullest account is of course that of John.

8. All four of them.

9. In Luke only: chapter 24.

10. You would be wrong if you gave any one of these answers. The ascension is recorded in Acts.

QUIZ AND PUZZLE BOOKS

Bible Acrostics, by W. Smith
Bible-Centered Crossword Puzzles,
  by C. E. Whitlow
Bible Clue Puzzle Book,
  by W. P. Keasbey
Bible Crossword Puzzle Book,
  by S. K. Davis
Bible Dial-a-Word, by G. DeYoung
Bible Facts in Crossword Puzzles,
  by F. Spencer
Bible Facts the Easy Way, by E. Filipi
Bible Key Word Quizzes,
  by J. G. Malphurs
Bible Number Quiz Book, by M. Stilson
Bible People in Crossword Puzzles,
  No. 2, by L. P. Johnson
Bible Puzzles for Adults,
  by G. Vander Klay
Bible Puzzles, Quizzes and Games,
  by H. Pettigrew
Bible Questions in Rhymes, Puzzles,
  Quizzes and Games, by M. O. Honors
Bible Quiz Book, by F. Hall
Bible Quizzes and Puzzles,
  by H. Pettigrew
Bible Quizzes for Everybody, by F. Hall
Bible, Quizzes, Jumbles, and Matches,
  by A. Ford
Bible Stories in Acrostic Puzzles,
  by S. Smith
Bible Word Quest, by H. Pettigrew
Bible Word Search, by W. C. Gordon
Build a Word Bible Puzzles,
  by M. Stilson
Creation Story in Acrostic Puzzles,
  by S. Smith
Criss Crossword Puzzles of Bible,
  by D. W. Thompson
Crossword Puzzles from Bible Verses,
  by Paul N. Jones
1500 Bible Quizzes, by A. R. Wells
1400 Bible Facts, by E. C. McKenzie

Go Till You Guess, by A. R. Wells
Intriguing Bible Puzzles,
  by Erma Reynolds
Know Your Bible Better Quiz Book,
  by F. Hall
Know Your Bible Quiz Book,
  by A. R. Wells
Know Your Hymns Quiz Book
  by F. Hall
Life of Christ in Crossword Puzzles,
  by L. P. Johnson
Miracles and Parables of the Bible in
  Crossword Puzzles, by L. P. Johnson
New Testament in Crossword Puzzles,
  by L. P. Johnson
Number Quizzes on the Bible,
  by V. Hutchcroft
Old Testament in Crossword Puzzles,
  by L. P. Johnson
Puzzle Fun with Bible Clues,
  by W. P. Keasbey
Quickie Quizzes from the Bible 1,
  by C. Vander Meer
Quickie Quizzes from Bible 2,
  by C. Vander Meer
Quiz Book on the Bible, by A. W. Kelly
Scripture-Based Crossword Puzzles,
  by G. Whitlow
Scripture Geometrics,
  by Jeffrey L. Fullman
Seek and Find Bible Puzzles,
  by M. Stilson
Teaching of Bible in Crossword Puzzles,
  by L. P. Johnson
Teachings of Christ in Crossword
  Puzzles, by L. P. Johnson
What Do You Know? Bible Quizzes,
  by V. Pewtress
When? Why? How? Bible Quizzes,
  by M. Stilson
Who? What? Where? Bible Quizzes,
  by M. Stilson

BAKER BOOK HOUSE
Grand Rapids, Michigan